EASY SPANISH PHRASE BOOK FOR TRAVELERS

Learn How to Speak Over 1400 Unique Spanish Words and Phrases While Traveling Spain and South America (Beginners Guide)

MATEO RAMIREZ

TABLE OF CONTENTS

INTRODUCTION

S panish and English share many, many things. Beyond cognates and a Latin base though, they differ in one very important area. Spanish is written phonetically, which for a beginning speaker, assists massively in day to day living: *If you can read it, you can say it.* From advertisements in the busy downtown streets to inscriptions on a local cathedral or church, your ability to speak and read Spanish are inextricably linked. Now, the first step to speaking any language is to learn the sounds, and because Spanish is phonetically written, that means turning first to the alphabet.

The Spanish Alphabet

In general, the Spanish alphabet should seem very familiar as the letters do not stray too far from the English alphabet:

AH (a), BAY (b), SAY [THAY, in Spain] (c), DAY (d), EY (e), EH-fay (f), HAY (g), AH-chay (h), EE (i), HOH-tah (j), KAH (k), EH-lay (l), EH-may (m), EH-nay (n), EH-nyay (ñ), OH (o), PAY (p), COO (q), EH-rray (r), EH-say (s), TAY (t), OOH (u), OOH-bay (v), DOH-blay OOH-bay (w), EH-kees (x), YAY (y), SAY-tah [THAY-tah, in Spain] (z).

The points of differentiation lay in the (ch), (ñ), (ll) and (rr) sounds—English does not possess these letters or sounds specifically. The sonics of the alphabet can be broken down simply:

a	... sounds like the "ah" sound used for a rush of understanding: "Ah, I understand!"
b	... typically sounds like an English "b".

1

	Depending on the dialect, though it can also come across as more of a "V"—the sounds are rather interchangeable (eg: "Vamos" = /bah-mohs/).
c	... often sounds like the English "k". Before "e" or "i", it sounds like an "s".
ch	... sounds like the "ch" in cheddar.
d	... sounds very similar to the English "d", except you should place your tongue against your upper teeth instead of the roof of your mouth when pronouncing it. It often sounds like the "th" in English "then", especially when it comes between two vowels.
e	... sounds like the reaction you might have when feeling unsure about something offered. "Do you want this? "Ehh, I guess so? Let me think about it."
f	... is the exact same in Spanish!
g	... often sounds just like an English "g". However, if it comes before and "e" or "i", it sounds more like the Spanish "j" (as described below).
h	... contributes no sound to the word unless if the word is foreign. For example, in Häagen Dazs, the "H" is pronounced.
i	... sounds like English "ee" but shorter.
j	... sounds different depending on the country! It will never sound like an English "j" however. Typically, it is more of a congested "h" sound stemming from the arabic roots in Spanish. Imagine the Hebrew "chutzpah", or if the word "Harold" was stuck in your throat.
k	... is very uncommon but sounds the same as

	an English "k" from "koala".
l	… is very similar to the English version! However, the tongue is slightly higher, resulting in a shorter sound.
ll	… sounds differently depending on the country. This is discussed more in depth in the section on dialects, but the sound is either a "y" sound as in "yellow" or a "sh" sound as in "shell".
m	… is the exact same in Spanish!
n	… is the exact same in Spanish too!
ñ	A completely separate letter from the English alphabet, the /enyeh/ sounds more like the "ny" in "canyon".
o	… sounds close to the "o" in "no" but shorter.
p	… sounds close to the English "p", but as if you're panting after a long sprint.
q	… sounds like the English "k", like in "que", pronounced /keh/. This letter is always followed by the letter "u".
r	… sounds a bit similar to the first "d" sound in the English word "daddy", but closer to the "tt" in "attic" than the "d" in "duck".
rr	… is very difficult for English speakers to learn because the tongue must move in an unfamiliar manner. A great way to practice is to say the word "butter" with an American accent. That middle sound, almost in between the t's, is what you're trying to say with this letter. Notice, this is not the same as "r"—to roll the "r" into the "rr" is akin to saying "n" instead of "m".
s	… is the exact same in Spanish!

t	... sounds like someone saying "tea" as they blow on hot tea. It sounds similar to the English "t" but without the violent ending, rather a gentle blow.
u	... sounds like the "oo" in the word "food" or "eu" in "leud".
v	... again, sounds more like an English "B" than a distinct sound itself (see **b**).
w	... sounds similar to the English "W". However, it is not a native Spanish letter and only used in foreign words (see **h**).
x	.. varies depending on the dialect; it is best to assume the sound of "ks" from the end of "socks" or the popping of a soda can.
y	... will sound like the "y" in "yes". However, if it is at the end of the word (eg: "hay"), it often sounds like a "i".
z	... is the exact same in Spanish! However, in some parts of Spain it is interchangeable with the English "c" and "s" sounds.

Understanding the Spanish alphabet is critical for gaining traction in the language as a whole. It is a quick and easy way to understand the phonetics of the entire language, something that most other large languages do not have. In particular, having a native speaker work through these sounds with you is a great way to develop a strong foundation in the language. Not only will it help you with using this book to its fullest potential, it will also allow for better and more authentic interactions in your travels!

CHAPTER ONE
COUNTRY SPECIFIC DIALECTS

Because English is so widely used around the world, it consists of many different dialects and accents. Beyond the traditional accents of native English speakers, those who speak Engligh as a secondary language add their countries' unique vernaculars, customs, and accents to the language as well. This idea is similar in Spanish; however it remains a poor analogy for the experience itself.

If an Englishman from South London and an American from Colorado are speaking to one another, there will be some confusion. *Pants* and *cookies* in the United States are not the same as in a British dialect. However, when a British person says *trousers* or *biscuits*, Americans are not thrown. Both of those words still appear in our lexicon; though they are not the first words that come up when describing these specific items (which would be *pants* and *cookies* respectively), they make sense in context.

This level of variation is ramped up in Spanish. Native Spanish speaking countries are completely different from one another, thousands and thousands of miles apart, and have minimal interactions with each other. Often, the words are simply different. For example, if you're getting breakfast in Mexico City and would like an avocado on the side, you might ask for an *aguacate*. But suppose you're late for a flight and have to run out the door, jump on the plane, and land 13 hours later in Buenos Aires. Still craving an avocado, you stop your taxi by a tienda and kindly ask for an *aguacate*. But it isn't an *aguacate* in Buenos Aires, it's a *palta*.

These two words have completely different origins, yet they represent the same thing. The changes do not stop with food—Venezuelans moving to either Mexico or Argentina must learn new words for clothing. Latin Americans moving to Spain must change the way they use certain verbs. It is important to study the vocabulary of the specific region or country you are visiting! While base verbs and phrases will remain the same, linguistic nuances within each country will show up.

The accents are similarly different throughout the various regions. Let's go through each of the different countries and see what's unique about them.

Argentina & Uruguay

Though they are very different places, Argentina and Uruguay share a very similar dialect known as Rioplatense. Rioplatense is a mixture of the traditional Castellano from Spain and other South American dialects, and it is characterized by a distinct accent and variable grammatical structure. There are a few things of note here.

1.   The use of *vos* instead of *tu*

The vosotros form is one of the many things carried over from Castellano Spanish. However, in Argentina and Uruguay, other than in literature, the rules regarding formal and informal grammatical forms are not as respected or used. While *vos* and *tu* both traditionally refer to the second-person *you*, *vos* being the formal title and *tu*, the informal, Argentina and Uruguay use *vos* for both. This is a small change to keep in mind.

2.   Changes to basic words that follow *vos*

As a result, there's a difference in the way words are pronounced in the second person (you/you're) singular tense. The emphasis shifts to the second half of the word, ending with force rather than sputtering out.

a. (You want) *Quieres* = *queres*

b. (You have) *Tienes* = *tenes*

c. (You can) *Puedes* = *podes*

d. (You are) *Eres* = *sos*

e. -ar verbs change from *-ar* to *-ás*

f. -er verbs change from *-er* to *-és*

g. -ir verbs change from *-ir* to *-ís*

3. Pronunciation of the *LL*

The most obvious and tell-tale sign that someone is from Argentina or Uruguay is how they pronounce the *LL*. Instead of pronouncing it like the English *y* sound, Argentines and Uruguayans pronounce *LL* like the English *sh*. The easiest example of this can be seen in the word *pollo*. The shifts from *(poh-yoh)* to *(poh-shoh)* becomes a consistent point of confusion for many tourists and visitors. This shift applies throughout the entire language—*Llaves (yah-beh)* becomes *(sha-vehs)* and *alla (ah-yah)* becomes *(ah-shah)*. Be careful around these! Although most likely you will still be understood pronouncing words as you see fit, understanding and comprehension may be affected dramatically!

Mexican Spanish

This particular dialect is prolific throughout the Southwestern United States as well as other countries surrounding Mexico. For Americans, it is the most recognizable Spanish accent simply due to proximity, and American English has adopted many local Spanish words such as *taco, cilantro,* and *sierra.* Americans are not the only one affected, however. Because of this proximity, Americanisms and various phrases have crept into the Spanish-indigenous conglomeration that had already previously absorbed Mexican Spanish. This results in a language sprinkled with English terms in conjunction to native terms—*computadora* and *rentar* are two cognates not originally used in Spain or other heavily Castellano-influenced dialects. Mexican Spanish does not use the *vosotros* form—rather it relies primarily on the *ustedes* (English: plural you as in "you all") endings.

It would be remiss to avoid the Mexican slang that makes up such a distinct part of the dialect. Words like *güey* and *chingón* are littered throughout many conversations and are typically used amicably to mean "friend" and "bad-ass" respectively. Another major term commonly said on the streets of Mexico is the word *mande* from *mandar* meaning "to command". This word is used in reaction to inquiry or introduction to command you, quite literally asking someone to tell you what to do. However, it is also used in Mexican Spanish in place of *Que* or *Como,* which follows an inquiry in other dialects.

Peru, Columbia, Ecuador, and Columbia

These countries have the easiest Spanish for beginners. The language here exists in highly diverse and indigenous cultures—the Spanish in other countries is a much slower, fully pronounced language that has native slang thrown into the mix. Hence, with exception to the various colloquialisms that comes up from time to time, these countries do a good job of never cutting words or diverging from the base language itself. There are two places of discrepancy, but they are very minor in their effect.

First, and the main source of confusion, is the slight *j* sound the accompanies the *y* and *ll*. Using a previous example, *pollo,* naturally pronounced *(poh-yoh),* is shifted slightly to *(poh-jyoh)* in these countries. The result is a dialect that comes off moderately different but ultimately very similar to other countries' dialects. *Llaves* become *(jya-vehs)* and *llamo* becomes *(jyah-moh).* By far, these are the most neutral accents in the Spanish speaking world. The locals in these countries speak slowly and work to pronounce every syllable, making the ideal environment for new speakers to learn and experience the language.

Guatemala, Honduras, Panama, Costa Rica, Nicaragua, and El Salvador

These countries retain a unique blend of South and North American Spanish. While each has its own specific dialect, the changes in language depend primarily on their closest, and hence most influential, Spanish speaking neighbor. For example, Guatemalan Spanish more closely resembles Mexican Spanish, while Panamanian Spanish more closely resembles Columbian Spanish.

One thing of note is the use of *vos* in this part of the world. Costa Rica, Nicaragua, and El Salvador use *vos* in a similar manner to Argentina and Uruguay. However, the use of the *vosotros* form does not expand past the common *vos* and respective conjugations.

The Carribean

There is a very significant difference between the Cuban, Puerto Rican, and Dominican accents, but they are all characterized by a few similarities. First of all, they are very, very fast-speaking dialects, acting as an inverse to the Peruvian or Columbian accent. From that restriction comes a shift in the pronunciation of overall words—Carribean accents sacrifice the full body of a word for the speed of saying it. This often means letters or entire syllables are left off the end of words, especially the most common ones. *"Como estas,"* pronounced *(koh-moh ehs-tahs)* in most other dialects, becomes *(koh-moh tah)*. Leaving off the *s* is not something reserved for the end of a phrase—often, the *s* in the middle of a word is also completely avoided. This is seen best in the word *estacion* which, pronounced typically as *(eh-stah-syon)*, is *(eh-tah-syoh)* in Carribean Spanish. Notice how both the ending of the word and the *s* in the middle are dropped off.

It is very common for the end or beginning of words to be cut off completely, specifically in the *estar* verb, leading to potentially confusing sentences even for native speakers. Further, there is often a shift of the subject-verb placement. Where other dialects might use *"donde vas tu?"*, Carribean native will say *"donde tu vas?"*, pronounced as *(dohn-deh teh bah)*.

Puerto Rican Spanish changes surrounding the letter *r* more than any other letter. An *r* at the end of a word, particularly if an infinitive, is often more strongly emphasized than in other dialects. Rather than the trailing off or soft nature of other forms, there is a shift in pronunciation towards the end of a word. Further, if an *r* falls in the middle of a word, it becomes more of an *l* sound. Words like *cambiar*, with only one *r*, shift toward an emphasis of the ending. On the other hand, something like *Puerto Rico* becomes more like *Puelto Rico*.

Carribean accents can be the most difficult for non-native speakers to understand. They are heavily influenced by African dialects that contain forms and phrases completely foreign to English-speaking ears. And as stated above, these shifts have expanded into the grammar and speed of the language. But fear not! These accents are full of life—they are fun to learn and will make speaking in other countries a breeze.

Chile

Though the country borders both Argentina and Peru, Chileans have an accent distinct from all other countries in the Spanish-speaking world. The rules of Chilean Spanish do not apply in any other dialect, involve the consistent removal of sounds within words, and is very difficult to understand without a familiarity with the dialect.

An immediate difference is the pronunciation of the *ch* as an *sh*. When asked where they are from, a Chilean will reply with (*shee-leh*). This is one of the easier and more obvious differences within the dialect. From there, most other shifts surround the inclusion of specific sounds in very fixed contexts.

Words ending in a vowel followed by *do* or *da*, as seen in many conjugations and adverbs, drop the distinction of the *d* sound at the end and then emphasize the vowel. As examples, words like *fundido* or *graduado* become *fundío* and *graduáo*. These words are difficult to pronounce and understand without having the signature *d* sound as an accompaniment because the precision of the final vowel's emphasis requires a trained ear familiar with its subtlety. If the Chilean *fundío* is pronounced *fundió*, it can change the meaning of the entire word or sentence.

Further, there is a blending of words and sounds throughout various pronunciations. This is most often caused by a dropped *d* at the beginning of words. But the *d* is only dropped if the following word ends with an *a* sound. A question like, "*¿dónde está la biblioteca?*" would become "*¿onde está la biblioteca?*" Further, words ending with the *von* drop the *v* sound in the middle. A perfect example of this is the word *huevon* (English: dude), which is pronounced (*hue'on*) in Chilean Spanish. Lastly, the all too common word *para* is often changed in a sentence based on the following verb's gender. If *para* is followed by an *el* or masculine verb, it is typically converted to a *pa'l*, pronounced like the *pal* in "palm". If the word following *para* is a *la* or feminine verb, *para* will become *pá la*, with a distinct emphasis on the *a*.

Learning Chilean Spanish can be a touch difficult because of these quirky pronunciations and changes to everyday language. Chileans are often discriminated against in international communities because of their accents—It is always important to be aware of what the accent says to other speakers!

Castilian Accent in Spain

Though Castile is the official birthplace of the Spanish language, it's dialect is significantly underwritten outside of Europe. Spain itself has many different and distinct dialects, but *Castillano* is recognised as the official and most common dialect within Spain.

The largest deviation of Castilian Spanish from other varieties stems grammatically from the *vosotros* form. This form is similar to the SouthEastern United States' "y'all", or the Irish "ye", by acting as a second person plural. While other dialects place this burden of communication on the *ustedes* form of the verb, Castilian Spanish does not. Imagine running into a group of friends. In Latin America, typically they would be addressed with a *"Como estan ustedes?"* (or simply *"Como estan?"*) Compare this to the Spanish *"Como estais?"*

Spaniards also are quick to use the imperfect subjunctive form, meaning that often the past tense can seem a little odd, even to native speakers. *Llegara*, the imperfect form of the verb *llegar* meaning "he/she arrived", is common throughout Latin America. But in Spain, *llegara* is more likely to be replaced with *llegarse*. While the meanings of these words are completely interchangeable, there are limitations to the overall flow and structure of the sentence with each verb conjugation!

The last thing that distinguishes "Spanish" from its Latin American counterparts lies in the overall accent. Spaniards are known for having a sort of lisp when they speak. This idea derives directly from their pronunciation of *z*, *ci*, and *ce* as an English *th*. The classic city of Barcelona is pronounced (*Bahr-seh-loh-nah*) by everyone outside of Spain. But inside the country, it becomes (*Bahr-theh-lohn-nah*). This distinction bleeds into other aspects of the language—it acts as more of a distinction rather than a difficulty when communicating. Absorbing this accent will quickly distinguish you from other dialects of Spanish more so than other accents.

Chapter Summary

- Each country has its own distinct accent that must be accommodated when traveling

- Speaking one country's dialect in another country is fine, but vocabulary, slang, and pronunciation will change

- Chilean and Carribean Spanish are the most difficult to understand for native speakers

CHAPTER TWO
WORDS YOU ALREADY KNOW

Abstract	Abstracto	*(ahbs-trahk-toh)*
Abstraction	Abstracción	*(ahbs-trahk-syohn)*
Academic	Académico	*(ah-kah-deh-mee-koh)*
Accusation	Acusación	*(ah-koo-sah-syohn)*
Act	Acto	*(ahk-toh)*
Action	Acción	*(ahk-syohn)*
Actor	Actor	*(ahk-duhr)*
Adaptation	Adaptación	*(ah-dahp-tah-syohn)*
Admirable	Admirable	*(ahd-muhr-uh-buhl)*
Admiration	Admiración	*(ahd-mee-rah-syohn)*
Agenda	Agenda	*(ah-hehn-dah)*
Alcohol	Alcohol	*(ahl-koh-ohl)*
Alcoholic	Alcohólico	*(ahl-koh-oh-lee-koh)*
Altar	Altar	*(ahl-tahr)*
Animal	Animal	*(ah-nee-mahl)*
Application	Aplicación	*(ah-plee-kah-syohn)*
Appreciation	Apreciación	*(ah-preh-syah-syohn)*
Area	Area	*(eh-ri-uh)*
Artefact	Artefacto	*(ahr-teh-fahk-toh)*

Artificial	Artificial	*(ar-dih-fih-shuhl)*
Artistic	Artístico	*(ahr-tees-tee-koh)*
Aspiration	Aspiración	*(ahs-pee-rah-syohn)*
Association	Asociación	*(ah-soh-syah-syohn)*
Attention	Atención	*(ah-tehn-syohn)*
Attraction	Atracción	*(ah-trahk-syohn)*
Authentic	Auténtico	*(ow-tehn-tee-koh)*
Authorization	Autorización	*(ow-toh-ree-sah-syohn)*
Auto	Auto	*(ow-toh)*
Automatic	Automático	*(ow-toh-mah-tee-koh)*
Balance	Balance	*(bah-lihns)*
Bar	Bar	*(bar)*
Base	Base	*(beys)*
Basic	Básico	*(bah-see-koh)*
Brutal	Brutal	*(bru-duhl)*
Cable	Cable	*(key-buhl)*
Canal	Canal	*(kah-nahl)*
Cancer	Cáncer	*(kahn-sehr)*
Canon	Canon	*(kah-nohn)*
Capital	Capital	*(kah-pee-tahl)*
Carbon	Carbón	*(kahr-bohn)*
Carton	Cartón	*(kahr-tohn)*
Celebration	Celebración	*(seh-leh-brah-syohn)*
Central	Central	*(sehn-trahl)*
Cerebral	Cerebral	*(sih-ri-bruhl)*

Characteristic	Característico	*(kah-rahk-teh-rees-tee-koh)*
Cheque	Cheque	*(cheh-keh)*
Chocolate	Chocolate	*(chak-liht)*
Circular	Circular	*(seer-koo-lahr)*
Circulation	Circulación	*(seer-koo-lah-syohn)*
Civil	Civil	*(see-beel)*
Civilization	Civilización	*(see-bee-lee-sah-syohn)*
Classic	Clásico	*(klah-see-koh)*
Classification	Clasificación	*(klah-see-fee-kah-syohn)*
Club	Club	*(kluhb)*
Collaboration	Colaboración	*(koh-lah-boh-rah-syohn)*
Collar	Collar	*(koh-yahr)*
Collection	Colección	*(koh-lehk-syohn)*
Colonial	Colonial	*(kuh-lo-ni-uhl)*
Coma	Coma	*(koh-mah)*
Combination	Combinación	*(kohm-bee-nah-syohn)*
Combustion	Combustión	*(kuhm-buhs-chihn)*
Comic	Cómico	*(koh-mee-koh)*
Compact	Compacto	*(kohm-pahk-toh)*
Compensation	Compensación	*(kohm-pehn-sah-syohn)*
Composition	Composición	*(kohm-poh-see-syohn)*

Concentration	Concentración	*(kohn-sehn-trah-syohn)*
Conception	Concepción	*(kohn-sehp-syohn)*
Conclusion	Conclusión	*(kohng-kloo-syohn)*
Condition	Condición	*(kohn-dee-syohn)*
Conductor	Conductor	*(kuhn-duhk-tuhr)*
Conflict	Conflicto	*(kohm-fleek-toh)*
Confusion	Confusión	*(kohm-foo-syohn)*
Conservation	Conservación	*(kohn-sehr-bah-syohn)*
Considerable	Considerable	*(kohn-see-deh-rah-bleh)*
Consideration	Consideración	*(kohn-see-deh-rah-syohn)*
Constitution	Constitución	*(kohns-tee-too-syohn)*
Construction	Construcción	*(kohns-trook-syohn)*
Contact	Contacto	*(kohn-tahk-toh)*
Control	Control	*(kuhn-trol)*
Cordial	Cordial	*(kohr-dyahl)*
Correct	Correcto	*(koh-rrehk-toh)*
Criminal	Criminal	*(krih-mih-nuhl)*
Crisis	Crisis	*(kree-sees)*
Cultural	Cultural	*(kool-too-rahl)*
Curious	Curioso	*(koo-ryoh-soh)*
Debate	Debate	*(dih-beyt)*
Decision	Decisión	*(deh-see-syohn)*
Delicious	Delicioso	*(deh-lee-syoh-soh)*

Democratic	Democrático	*(deh-moh-krah-tee-koh)*
Diagonal	Diagonal	*(day-ah-guh-nuhl)*
Dimension	Dimension	*(dih-mehn-shihn)*
Diplomatic	Diplomático	*(dee-ploh-mah-tee-koh)*
Director	Director	*(dee-rehk-tohr)*
Disco	Disco	*(dees-koh)*
Division	División	*(dee-bee-syohn)*
Doctor	Doctor	*(dak-duhr)*
Domestic	Doméstico	*(doh-mehs-tee-koh)*
Drama	Drama	*(dra-muh)*
Dramatic	Dramático	*(drah-mah-tee-koh)*
Dynamic	Dinámico	*(dee-nah-mee-koh)*
Economic	Económico	*(eh-koh-noh-mee-koh)*
Editorial	Editorial	*(eh-dee-toh-ryahl)*
Electoral	Electoral	*(eh-lehk-to-ral)*
Electronic	Electrónico	*(eh-lehk-troh-nee-koh)*
Elemental	Elemental	*(eh-leh-mehn-tahl)*
Enigma	Enigma	*(eh-nihg-muh)*
Erotic	Erótico	*(eh-roh-tee-koh)*
Error	Error	*(eh-rrohr)*
Exact	Exacto	*(ehk-sahk-toh)*
Except	Excepto	*(ehk-sehp-toh)*
Exclusive	Exclusive	*(ehk-sklu-sihv)*
Excursion	Excursion	*(ehk-skuhr-zhihn)*
Exotic	Exótico	*(ehk-soh-tee-koh)*

Experimental	Experimental	*(ehks-peh-ree-mehn-tahl)*
Explosion	Explosión	*(ehks-ploh-syohn)*
Exposition	Exposición	*(ehks-poh-see-syohn)*
Expulsion	Expulsion	*(ehks-pool-syohn)*
Extension	Extensión	*(ehks-tehn-syohn)*
Exterior	Exterior	*(ehks-teh-ryohr)*
Factor	Factor	*(fahk-tohr)*
Familiar	Familiar	*(fuh-mihl-yuhr)*
Fantastic	Fantástico	*(fahn-tahs-tee-koh)*
Fatal	Fatal	*(fah-tahl)*
Federal	Federal	*(feh-duh-ruhl)*
Festival	Festival	*(fehst-ih-vuhl)*
Fiction	Ficción	*(feek-syohn)*
Final	Final	*(fee-nahl)*
Flexible	Flexible	*(flehk-see-bleh)*
Formal	Formal	*(fohr-mahl)*
Formation	Formación	*(fohr-mah-syohn)*
Formula	Formula	*(fawr-myu-luh)*
Frontal	Frontal	*(frohn-tahl)*
Fundamental	Fundamental	*(fuhn-duh-mehn-tuhl)*
Gala	Gala	*(gah-lah)*
Gas	Gas	*(gahs)*
General	General	*(jehn-uhr-uhl)*
Generic	Genérico	*(heh-neh-ree-koh)*
Genesis	Génesis	*(heh-neh-sees)*

Geometric	Geométrico	*(hehoh-meh-tree-koh)*
Global	Global	*(gloh-bahl)*
Glorious	Glorioso	*(gloh-ryoh-soh)*
Grave	Grave	*(grah-beh)*
Habitual	Habitual	*(ah-bee-twahl)*
Heroic	Heroico	*(eh-roy-koh)*
Hobby	Hobby	*(hoh-bee)*
Horror	Horror	*(oh-rrohr)*
Hospital	Hospital	*(ohs-pee-tahl)*
Hotel	Hotel	*(ho-tel)*
Idea	Idea	*(ee-deh-ah)*
Ideal	Ideal	*(ee-deh-ahl)*
Imperial	Imperial	*(eem-peh-ryahl)*
Implacable	Implacable	*(eem-plah-kah-bleh)*
Individual	Individual	*(ihn-dih-vihj-u-uhl)*
Industrial	Industrial	*(een-doos-tryahl)*
Inevitable	Inevitable	*(ihn-ehv-uh-duh-buhl)*
Inferior	Inferior	*(eem-feh-ryohr)*
Informal	Informal	*(eem-fohr-mahl)*
Informative	Informative	*(ihn-fawr-muh-dihv)*
Insect	Insecto	*(een-sehk-toh)*
Inseparable	Inseparable	*(een-seh-pah-rah-bleh)*
Inspector	Inspector	*(eens-pehk-tohr)*

Interminable	Interminable	*(een-tehr-mee-nah-bleh)*
Invasion	Invasión	*(eem-bah-syohn)*
Invisible	Invisible	*(eem-bee-see-bleh)*
Ironic	Irónico	*(ee-roh-nee-koh)*
Irregular	Irregular	*(ee-rreh-goo-lahr)*
Judicial	Judicial	*(hoo-dee-syahl)*
Kilo	Kilo	*(kee-loh)*
Lateral	Lateral	*(lah-teh-rahl)*
Legal	Legal	*(leh-gahl)*
Liberal	Liberal	*(lee-beh-rahl)*
Literal	Literal	*(lih-duhr-uhl)*
Local	Local	*(lo-kuhl)*
Macho	Macho	*(mah-choh)*
Maestro	Maestro	*(mah-ehs-troh)*
Magic	Mágico	*(mah-hee-koh)*
Mango	Mango	*(mahng-goh)*
Mania	Manía	*(mah-nee-ah)*
Manual	Manual	*(mah-nwahl)*
Marginal	Marginal	*(mahr-hee-nahl)*
Mate	Mate	*(meyt)*
Material	Material	*(muh-tir-i-uhl)*
Matrimonial	Matrimonial	*(mah-tree-moh-nyahl)*
Medic	Médico	*(meh-dee-koh)*
Medieval	Medieval	*(mihd-i-vuhl)*
Mediocre	Mediocre	*(meh-dyoh-kreh)*
Melon	Melon	*(meh-lihn)*
Mental	Mental	*(mehn-tuhl)*

Menu	Menú	*(meh-noo)*
Metal	Metal	*(meh-duhl)*
Miserable	Miserable	*(mihz-ruh-buhl)*
Moral	Moral	*(moh-rahl)*
Mortal	Mortal	*(mohr-tahl)*
Mosaic	Mosaico	*(moh-say-koh)*
Motel	Motel	*(mo-tehl)*
Motor	Motor	*(mo-duhr)*
Multiple	Múltiple	*(mool-tee-pleh)*
Municipal	Municipal	*(moo-nee-see-pahl)*
Musical	Musical	*(myu-zih-kuhl)*
Mysterious	Misterioso	*(mees-teh-ryoh-soh)*
Nation	Nación	*(nah-syohn)*
Natural	Natural	*(nah-too-rahl)*
Noble	Noble	*(no-buhl)*
Normal	Normal	*(nawr-muhl)*
Nostalgia	Nostalgia	*(nohs-tahl-hyah)*
Numerous	Numeroso	*(noo-meh-roh-soh)*
Ópera	Ópera	*(oh-peh-rah)*
Oral	Oral	*(awr-uhl)*
Organic	Orgánico	*(ohr-gah-nee-koh)*
Oriental	Oriental	*(oh-ryehn-tahl)*
Original	Original	*(oh-ree-hee-nahl)*
Panic	Pánico	*(pah-nee-koh)*
Panorama	Panorama	*(pah-noh-rah-mah)*
Particular	Particular	*(par-tihk-yu-luhr)*
Pasta	Pasta	*(pahs-tah)*
Pastor	Pastor	*(pahs-tohr)*

Patio	Patio	*(pah-tyoh)*
Patron	Patrón	*(pah-trohn)*
Peculiar	Peculiar	*(pih-kyu-lyuhr)*
Penal	Penal	*(peh-nahl)*
Perfect	Perfecto	*(pehr-fehk-toh)*
Perfume	Perfume	*(puhr-fyum)*
Personal	Personal	*(pehr-soh-nahl)*
Peseta	Peseta	*(peh-seh-tah)*
Piano	Piano	*(pi-ahn-o)*
Plastic	Plástico	*(plahs-tee-koh)*
Plaza	Plaza	*(plah-sah)*
Plural	Plural	*(ploo-rahl)*
Poetic	Poético	*(poh-eh-tee-koh)*
Popular	Popular	*(poh-poo-lahr)*
Precious	Precioso	*(preh-syoh-soh)*
Pretension	Pretension	*(preh-tehn-syohn)*
Principal	Principal	*(preen-see-pahl)*
Probable	Probable	*(proh-bah-bleh)*
Product	Producto	*(proh-dook-toh)*
Propaganda	Propaganda	*(proh-pah-gahn-dah)*
Protector	Protector	*(proh-tehk-tohr)*
Provincial	Provincial	*(proh-been-syahl)*
Public	Público	*(poo-blee-koh)*
Radical	Radical	*(rrah-dee-kahl)*
Radio	Radio	*(rey-di-o)*
Region	Región	*(rreh-hyohn)*
Regular	Regular	*(rreh-goo-lahr)*

Religion	Religión	*(rreh-lee-hyohn)*
Religious	Religioso	*(rreh-lee-hyoh-soh)*
Reunion	Reunión	*(rreyoo-nyohn)*
Revision	Revision	*(rih-vih-zhihn)*
Ritual	Ritual	*(rih-chu-uhl)*
Romantic	Romántico	*(rroh-mahn-tee-koh)*
Rural	Rural	*(rroo-rahl)*
Secular	Secular	*(seh-koo-lahr)*
Sentimental	Sentimental	*(sehn-tee-mehn-tahl)*
Serial	Serial	*(si-ri-uhl)*
Sexual	Sexual	*(sehk-shu-uhl)*
Similar	Similar	*(sih-muh-luhr)*
Simple	Simple	*(sihm-puhl)*
Singular	Singular	*(seeng-goo-lahr)*
Social	Social	*(so-shuhl)*
Solar	Solar	*(soh-lahr)*
Solo	Solo	*(soh-loh)*
Superficial	Superficial	*(soo-pehr-fee-syahl)*
Superior	Superior	*(suh-pir-i-uhr)*
Taxi	Taxi	*(tahk-si)*
Tedious	Tedioso	*(teh-dyoh-soh)*
Television	Televisión	*(teh-leh-bee-syohn)*
Terrible	Terrible	*(teh-ruh-buhl)*
Terror	Terror	*(tehr-uhr)*
Total	Total	*(toh-tahl)*
Tragic	Trágico	*(trah-hee-koh)*

Transcendental	Transcendental	*(trah-sehn-dehn-tahl)*
Triple	Triple	*(tree-pleh)*
Tropical	Tropical	*(troh-pee-kahl)*
Unión	Unión	*(oo-nyohn)*
Universal	Universal	*(oo-nee-behr-sahl)*
Usual	Usual	*(oo-swahl)*
Verbal	Verbal	*(behr-bahl)*
Version	Versión	*(behr-syohn)*
Vertical	Vertical	*(behr-tee-kahl)*
Violin	Violín	*(byoh-leen)*
Visible	Visible	*(bee-see-bleh)*
Visual	Visual	*(bee-swahl)*
Vital	Vital	*(vay-duhl)*
Vulgar	Vulgar	*(vul-gar)*
Vulnerable	Vulnerable	*(bool-neh-rah-bleh)*

CHAPTER THREE
BASIC CONVERSATION

Greetings

Hello	Hola	*(oh-lah)*
How are you?	¿Qué tal?	*(keh tahl)*
How are you?	¿Cómo estas?	*(koh-moh ehs-tahs)*
What's up?	¿Qué pasa?	*(keh pah-sah)*
How're you doing?	¿Cómo te va?	*(koh-moh teh va)*
Good	Bien	*(byehn)*
Very good	Muy bien	*(mwee byehn)*
Great	Buenísimo	*(boen-eese-e-mo)*
So-so	Así así	*(ah-see ah-see)*
Not so good	No tan bien	*(noh tahn byehn)*
And you?	¿Y tú?	*(ee too)*
My name is…	Me llamo…	*(meh yamoh)*
What's your name?	¿Cómo te llamas?	*(koh-moh teh yamahs?)*
I am…	Soy…	*(soy)*
What is your name?	¿Cuál es tu nombre?	*(kwahl ehs too nohm-breh)*
Nice to meet you	Mucho gusto	*(moo-choh goos-toh)*
A pleasure!	Un gusto	*(oon goos-toh)*
A pleasure	Placér	*(plass-ehr)*
Charmed, Likewise	Encantado/Encantada	*(ehng-kahn-tah-doh/dah)*

Polite Phrases

Thank you	Gracias	*(grah-syahs)*
You're welcome	De nada	*(deh nah-dah)*
No problem	No hay de qué	*(noh ay deh keh)*
Excuse me	Disculpe	*(dees-kool-peh)*
Pardon me	Perdón	*(pahrdohn-eh)*
I'm sorry	Lo siento	*(loh see-entoh)*

Common Questions

Where's the bathroom?	¿Dónde está el baño?	*(Dohn-deh ehs-tah el ban-yo)*
What time is it?	¿Qué hora es?	*(keh oh-rah es)*
Is something wrong?	¿Pasa algo?	*(pah-sah ahl-goh)*
Is this right?	¿Es esto correcto?	*(es ehs-toh koh-rrehk-toh)*
Was I wrong?	¿Me equivocado?	*(meh eh-kee-boh-kah-doh)*
Can you help me with this?	¿Me puede ayudar con esto?	*(meh pweh-deh ah-yoo-dahr kohn ehs-toh)*
Can you bring me ... please?	¿Puedes traerme ... por favor?	*(pweh-dehs trah-ehr-meh ... pohr fahbohr)*
Can I come in?	¿Puedo entrar?	*(pweh-doh ehn-trahr)*
Want to grab a drink?	¿Quieres tomar una copa?	*(kyeh-rehs toh-mar oo-nah coh-pah)*

Where should we go to eat?	¿A dónde deberíamos ir a comer?	*(ah dohn-deh dehber-reeahn-mos eer ah koh-mehr)*
Are you ready?	¿Estás listo?	*(ehs-tahs lees-toh)*

Common Replies

Fine, thank you	Muy bien, gracias	*(mwee byehn, grah-syahs)*
You're welcome	De nada	*(deh nah-dah)*
Yes	Sí	*(see)*
No	No	*(noh)*
Long time no see!	¡Cuánto tiempo sin verlo/a!	*(kwahn-toh tyehm-poh seen vehrloh/lah)*
Good luck!	¡Buena suerte!	*(Bweh-nah swehr-teh)*
Stop!	¡Alto!	*(Alh-toh)*
Cheers!	¡Salud!	*(sah-lood)*
Get well soon	Que te mejores	*(keh teh mehores)*
Bon appetit	Buen provecho	*(bwehn proh-beh-choh)*
Take care	Cuídate	*(kwee-dah-teh)*
Congratulations	Felicitaciones	*(feh-lee-see-tah-siohnes)*
Well done!	¡Bien hecho!	*(byehn eh-choh)*
Genius!	¡Genio!	*(heh-nyoh)*
Stupendous	Estupendo	*(ehs-too-pen-doh)*
Awesome	Genial	*(heh-nyahl)*

Incredible!	¡Increíble!	*(eeng-kreh-ee-bleh)*

Goodbyes

See you tomorrow	Nos vemos mañana	*(Nos veh-mos mah-nyah-nah)*
See you later	Hasta luego	*(ahs-tah lweh-goh)*
See you soon, friend	Hasta pronto amigo	*(ahs-tah prohn-toh ah-mee-goh)*
Goodbye, friend!	Ciao, amigo!	*(chau ah-mee-goh)*

More Basics

there is / is there	Hay	*(ay)*
you have / have you?	Tiene	*(tee-ehneh)*
I want	Quiero	*(kyeh-roh)*
I have	Tengo	*(tehn-goh)*

CHAPTER FOUR
MONEY, TIME, AND COUNTING

Money

Bank	Banco	*(bahng-koh)*
Money	Dinero	*(dih-nehr-o)*
Change / Exchange	Cambio	*(kahm-byoh)*
Traveler's Check	Cheque de viajero	*(cheh-keh deh byah-heh-roh)*
Bill	Billete de banco	*(bee-yeh-teh deh bahng-koh)*
Coins	Monedas	*(moh-neh-dah)*
Exchange rate	El tipo de cambio	*(tee-poh deh kahm-byoh)*
Commission	Comisión	*(koh-mee-syohn)*
Dollar	Dólar	*(doh-lahr)*
Pounds	Libras	*(lee-brahr)*
Euros	Euros	*(eyoo-roh)*
It costs $2	Cuesta dos dólares.	*(kwehs-tah dohs doh-lahr-es)*
It costs $39.99	Cuesta treinta y nueve dólares y noventa y nueve centavos	*(kwehs-tah treyn-tah ee nweh-beh doh-lahr-ez ee noh-behn-tah ee nweh-beh sehn-tah-boh)*
Three cents	Tres centavos	*(trehs sehn-tah-boh)*

Telling Time

It's one'o'clock	Es la una	*(Es lah oo-nah)*
It's two'o'clock	Son las dos	*(Sohn lahs dohs)*
It's three'o'clock	Son las tres	*(Sohn lahs trehs)*
It's four'o'clock	Son las cuatro	*(Sohn lahs kwah-troh)*
It's five'o'clock	Son las cinco	*(Sohn lahs seeng-koh)*
It's six'o'clock	Son las seis	*(Sohn lahs sayhs)*
It's seven'o'clock	Son las siete	*(Sohn lahs syeh-teh)*
It's eight'o'clock	Son las ocho	*(Sohn lahs oh-choh)*
It's nine'o'clock	Son las nueve	*(Sohn lahs nweh-beh)*
It's ten'o'clock	Son las diez	*(Sohn lahs dyehs)*
It's eleven'o'clock	Son las once	*(Sohn lahs ohnseh)*
It's twelve'o'clock	Son las doce	*(Sohn lahs dohseh)*
It's noon / midday	Es el mediodía	*(Es ehl meh-dyoh-dee-ah)*
It's midnight	Es la medianoche	*(Es la meh-dyah-noh-cheh)*
It's two in the morning	Son las dos de la mañana	*(Sohn lahs dohs deh lah mah-nyah-nah)*
It's two in the afternoon	Son las dos de la tarde	*(Sohn lahs dohs deh lah tahr-deh)*
It's eight in the evening	Son las ocho de la noche	*(Sohn lahs ohchoh deh lah noh-cheh)*
It's one forty	Es la una y cuarenta	*(Es lah oo-nah ee kwah-rehn-tah)*

It's twenty minutes to two	Son las dos menos veinte	*(Sohn lahs dohs meh-nohs beyn-teh)*
It's one forty-five	Es la una y cuarenta y cinco	*(Es lah oo-nah ee kwah-rehn-tah ee seeng-koh)*
It's a quarter to two	Son las dos menos cuarto	*(Sohn lahs dohs meh-nohs kwahr-toh)*
It's ten past two	Son las dos y diez	*(Sohn lahs dohs ee dyehs)*
It's quarter past two	Son las dos y cuarto	*(Sohn lahs dohs ee kwahr-toh)*
It's half past two	Son las dos y media	*(Sohn lahs dohs ee meh-dyah)*
I have my Spanish class at five	Tengo mi clase de español a las cinco	*(tehn-goh mee klah-seh deh ehs-pah-nyohl ah lahs seeng-koh)*
Shall we meet at seven?	¿Nos encontramos a las siete?	*(nohs ehn-kohn-trah-mos ah lah see-eteh)*
When is sunset?	¿Cuándo es atardecer?	*(kwahn-doh es ah-tahr-deh-sehr)*
When is sunrise?	¿Cuándo es el amanecer?	*(kwahn-doh es el ah-mah-neh-sehr)*
Where is the Museum of Natural History?	¿Dónde está el Museo de Ciencias Naturales?	*(dohn-deh ehs-tah el moo-seh-oh deh ees-toh-ryah nah-too-rahl)*
Where is ____ Avenue?	¿Dónde está la Avenida _____?	*(dohn-deh ehs-tah lah ah-beh-nee-dah ____)*
Where is a pharmacy?	¿Dónde hay una farmacia?	*(dohn-deh ay oon-ah fahr-mah-syah)*

Basic Numbers

1	uno	*(unoh)*
2	dos	*(dohs)*
3	tres	*(trehs)*
4	cuatro	*(kwah-troh)*
5	cinco	*(seeng-koh)*
6	seis	*(seys)*
7	siete	*(syeh-teh)*
8	ocho	*(oh-choh)*
9	nueve	*(nweh-beh)*
10	diez	*(dyehs)*
11	once	*(ohn-seh)*
12	doce	*(doh-seh)*
13	trece	*(treh-seh)*
14	catorce	*(kah-tohr-seh)*
15	quince	*(keen-seh)*
16	dieciséis	*(dyeh-see-seys)*
17	diecisiete	*(dyeh-see-syeh-teh)*
18	dieciocho	*(dyeh-see-oh-choh)*
19	diecinueve	*(dyeh-see-nweh-beh)*
20	veinte	*(beyn-teh)*
21	veintiuno	*(behn-tyoo-noh)*
22	veintidós	*(beyn-tee-dohs)*
23	veintitrés	*(beyn-tee-trehs)*
24	veinticuatro	*(beyn-tee-kwah-troh)*

25	veinticinco	*(beyn-tee-seeng-koh)*
26	veintiséis	*(beyn-tee-seys)*
27	veintisiete	*(beyn-tee-syeh-teh)*
28	veintiocho	*(beyn-tee-oh-choh)*
29	veintinueve	*(beyn-tee-nweh-beh)*
30	treinta	*(treyn-tah)*
31	treinta y uno	*(treyn-tah ee oo-noh)*
32	treinta y dos	*(treyn-tah ee dohs)*
33	treinta y tres	*(treyn-tah ee trehs)*
40	cuarenta	*(kwah-rehn-tah)*
41	cuarenta y uno	*(kwah-rehn-tah ee oo-noh)*
42	cuarenta y dos	*(kwah-rehn-tah ee dohs)*
50	cincuenta	*(seeng-kwehn-tah)*
67	sesenta	*(seh-sehn-tah)*
70	setenta	*(seh-tehn-tah)*
80	ochenta	*(oh-chehn-tah)*
90	noventa	*(noh-behn-tah)*
100	cien	*(syehn)*
101	ciento uno	*(syehn-toh oo-noh)*
102	ciento dos	*(syehn-toh dohs)*
110	ciento diez	*(syehn-toh dyehs)*
111	ciento once	*(syehn-toh ohn-seh)*
200	doscientos	*(dohs-syehn-tohs)*
201	doscientos uno	*(dohs-syehn-tohs oo-noh)*
202	doscientos dos	*(dohs-syehn-tohs dohs)*

211	doscientos once	*(dohs-syehn-tohs ohn-seh)*
276	doscientos setenta y seis	*(dohs-syehn-tohs setenta ee seys)*
300	trescientos	*(trehs-syehn-tohs)*
400	cuatrociento s	*(kwah-troh-syehn-tohs)*
500	quinientos	*(kee-nyehn-tohs)*
600	seiscientos	*(sey-syehn-tohs)*
700	setecientos	*(seh-teh-syehn-tohs)*
800	ochocientos	*(oh-choh-syehn-tohs)*
900	novecientos	*(noh-beh-syehn-tohs)*
1000	mil	*(meel)*
1011	mil once	*(meel ohn-seh)*
1111	mil ciento once	*(meel syehn-toh ohn-seh)*
2000	dos mil	*(dohs meel)*
3000003	tres millones tres	*(trehs mee-yohn trehs)*

CHAPTER FIVE
EARLY ORIENTATION

Weather

It is hot	Hace calor	*(ah-seh kah-lohr)*
It is cold	Hace frío	*(ah-seh free-oh)*
It is cool	Hace fresco	*(ah-seh frehs-koh)*
The weather is nice	Hace buen tiempo	*(ah-seh bwehn tyehm-poh)*
The weather is bad	Hace mal tiempo	*(ah-seh mahl tyehm-poh)*
It is cloudy	Está nublado	*(ehs-tah noo-blah-doh)*
It is sunny	Está soleado	*(ehs-tah soh-leh-ah-doh)*
It is clear	Está despejado	*(ehs-tah dehs-peh-hah-doh)*
It is windy	Está ventoso	*(ehs-tah behn-toh-soh)*
It is stormy	Está tormentoso	*(ehs-tah tohr-mehn-toh-soh)*
It is raining	Está lloviendo	*(ehs-tah yoh-be-endoh)*
It is snowing	Está nevando	*(ehs-tah neh-bandoh)*
It's windy	Hay viento	*(ay byehn-toh)*
It is foggy	Hay niebla	*(ay nyeh-blah)*
It's raining pitchers/buckets!	¡Llueve a cántaros!	*(yuh-eh-beh ah kahn-tah-rohs)*
It's raining oceans!	¡Llueve a mares!	*(yuh-eh-beh ah mahr-ehs)*

Whenever it rained, it stopped	Siempre que llovió, paró	*(syehm-preh keh yoh-beoh,pah-roh)*
It's so cold it burns your skin!	¡Hace un frío que pela!	*(ah-seh oon free-oh keh peh-lah)*
I'm freezing!	¡Me estoy congelando!	*(meh ehs-toy kohng-heh-landoh)*
What heat!	¡Ay, qué calor!	*(ay keh kah-lohr)*
It's an oven!	¡Es un horno!	*(es oon ohr-noh)*

Customs

Your passport please.	Su pasaporte, por favor.	*(soo pah-sah-pohr-teh, pohr fah-bohr)*
Here is my passport.	Aquí está mi pasaporte.	*(ah-kee ehs-tah mee pah-sah-pohr-teh)*
Do you have anything to declare?	¿Tiene algo declarar?	*(tee-ehneh ahl-goh deh-klah-rahr)*
I have nothing to declare.	No tengo nada declarar.	*(noh tehn-goh nahdah deh-klah-rahr)*
Is this your baggage?	¿Es ésta su equipaje?	*(Es ehs-tah soo eh-kee-pah-heh)*
This is my suitcase.	Aquí está mi valija.	*(ah-kee ehs-tah mee bah-lee-hah)*

How long do you intend to stay here?	¿Cuánto tiempo piensa estar aquí?	*(kwahn-toh tyehm-poh pehn-sah eh-stahr ah-kee)*
I'll be staying here a few days.	Estaré aquí unos días.	*(eh-stahreh ah-kee oo-nohs dey-ahs)*
I'll be staying here a month.	Estaré aquí un més.	*(eh-stahreh ah-kee oon mehs)*
I'll be staying here a week.	Estaré aquí una semana.	*(eh-stahreh ah-kee oo-nah seh-mah-nah)*
I'm here in transit (only passing through).	Estoy aquí de tránsito.	*(ehs-tohy ah-kee deh trahn-see-toh)*
What is the purpose of your visit?	¿Cual es el propósito de su visita?	*(kwahl es el proh-poh-see-toh deh soo bee-see-tah)*
I'm here on vacation.	Estoy aquí de vacaciones.	*(ehs-tohy ah-kee deh bah-kah-syohn-ehs)*
I'm here on business.	Estoy aquí en viaje de negocios.	*(ehs-tohy ah-kee en byah-heh deh neh-goh-syohsdeh bah-kah-syohn-ehs)*
May I go?	¿Puedo irme?	*(pweh-doh eer-meh)*

Exchanging Money

Where can I buy traveler's checks?	¿Donde puedo comprar cheques de viajero?	*(dohn-deh pweh-doh kohm-prahr cheh-kehs deh byah-heh-roh)*
Where can I change money?	¿Donde puedo cambiar dinero?	*(dohn-deh pweh-doh kahm-byahr dee-neh-roh)*
The bank is open from 9 to 5.	El banco está abierto de las 9 hasta las 5	*(ehl ban-koh ehs-tah ah-byehr-toh deh lahs nweh-beh ahs-tah lahs seeng-koh)*
Do you know where I can cash this check?	¿Sabe usted dónde puedo cambiar este cheque?	*(sah-beh oos-tehd dohn-deh pweh-doh kahm-byahr ehs-teh cheh-kehs)*
How many pesos can I buy for one dollar?	¿Cuantos pesos puedo comprar por un dólar?	*(kwahn-toh peh-sohs pweh-doh kohm-prahr pohr oon doh-lahr)*
We need to see some identification	Necesitamos ver alguna identificación	*(neh-seh-see-tah-mohs behr ahl-goo-nah ee-dehn-tee-fee-kah-syohn)*
You have to sign this paper here.	Usted tiene que firmar este papel aqui.	*(oos-tehd tyeh-neh keh feer-mahr ehs-teh pah-pehl ah-kee)*
Where do I have to sign?	¿Donde necesito firmar?	*(dohn-deh neh-seh-see-toh feer-mahr)*

The currency exchange is open.	Está abierto la oficina de cambio	*(estah ah-byehr-toh lah oh-fee-see-nah deh kahm-byoh)*
I need some coins too, please.	Nesecito algunas monedas también, por favor.	*(neh-seh-see-toh ahl-goo-nahs moh-neh-dah tahm-byehn, pohr fah-bohr)*
I'd like to cash a personal check.	Me gustaria cambiar un cheque personal.	*(meh goos-tahr-reeah kahm-byahr oon cheh-kehs pehr-soh-nahl)*
How much is the service charge to exchange money?	¿Cuanto es el cargo de servicio para cambiar dinero?	*(kwahn-toh ehs ehl kahr-goh deh sehr-bee-syoh pah-rah kahm-byahr dee-neh-roh)*

Finding Transportation

Is there a bus to the city's center?	¿Hay un autobús al centro?	*(ay oon ow-toh-boos ahl sehn-troh)*
I need a taxi to the ___ Hotel.	Necesito un taxi al Hotel ___.	*(neh-seh-see-toh oon tahk-see ahl oh-tehl)*
Can you please help me. I am lost.	¿Podría ayudarme? Me he perdido.	*(poh-dree-ah ah-yoo-dahr-meh? meh eh pehr-dee-doh)*

CHAPTER SIX
NAVIGATION

General Direction

Across from the park	En frente de la plaza	*(ehn frehn-teh deh lah plah-sah)*
Next to the gas station	Al lado de la gasolinera	*(Ahl lah-doh deh lah gah-soh-lee-neh-rah)*
Behind the theater	Detrás del teatro	*(deh-trahs dehl teh-ah-troh)*
Between the pharmacy and the post office	Entre la farmacia y el correo	*(ehn-treh lah fahr-mah-syah ee ehl koh-rreh-oh)*
On the corner	En la esquina	*(ehn lah ehs-kee-nah)*
Two blocks (from here)	A dos cuadras	*(ah dohs kwah-drahr)*
Ten minutes (from here)	A diez minutos	*(ah dyehs mee-noo-tohs)*
It's the next one	Es la próxima	*(ehs lah prohk-see-moh)*
It's the first one	Es la primera	*(ehs lah pree-mehr-ah)*
It's the second one	Es la segunda	*(ehs lah seh-goon-dah)*
It's the third one	Es la tercera	*(ehs lah tehr-seh-rah)*
Turn left	Dobla a la izquierda	*(doh-blah ah lah ees-kyehr-dah)*
Turn left	Gira a la izquierda	*(heer-ah ah lah ees-kyehr-dah)*

Turn right	Gira a la derecha	*(heer-ah ah lah deh-reh-chah)*
Turn right	Dobla a la derecha	*(doh-blah ah lah deh-reh-chah)*
Take/walk along...	Ve por..	*(veh pohr...)*
Cross...	Cruza...	*(kroo-sah)*
Continue / follow...	Sigue...	*(seh-geer)*
Go straight ahead	Sigue derecho	*(seh-geer deh-reh-choh)*

Navigation Questions

Where is the nearest bus stop?	¿Dónde está la parada de autobús más cerca?	*(dohn-deh est-ah lah pah-rah-dah ow-toh-boos mahs sehr-kah)*
How much does a ticket cost for ... ?	¿Cuánto cuesta un boleto para ... ?	*(kwahn-toh kwehs-tah oon boh-leh-toh pah-rah...?)*
Where can I find a taxi?	¿Dónde puedo encontrar un taxi?	*(dohn-deh pweh-doh ehn-kohn-trahr oon takh-see)*
Where can I find the train station?	¿Dónde puedo encontrar la estación de tren?	*(dohn-deh pweh-doh ehn-kohn-trahr lah ehs-tah-syohn deh trehn)*
How do I get to the ... ?	¿Cómo llego al/ a la ... ?	*(coh-moh yeh-goh ehl/ ah lah...)*
How far is the ... from the ... ?	¿Qué tan lejos queda el/la ... del/de la ... ?	*(keh tahn lehohs kay-dah ehl/ lah... dehl/ deh lah...)*

Is there a ... around here?	¿Hay un/una ... cerca de aquí?	*(ay oon/oonah... sehr-kah deh ah-kee)*
I think I'm lost.	Creo que estoy perdido/a.	*(kreh-oh keh ehs-tohy pehr-dee-doh/dah)*
Do you know if it's around here?	¿Sabes si está por aquí?	*(sah-behs see ehstah pohr ah-kee)*
Does the bus to ... pass by here?	¿Pasa por aquí el camión que va a ... ?	*(pah-sah pohr ah-kee ehl kah-myohn keh vah ah...)*
Where can I take a taxi?	¿Dónde puedo tomar un taxi?	*(dohn-deh pweh-doh toh-mahr uhn tahk-see)*

Asking for Directions

How do I get to...?	¿Cómo puedo ir a....?	*(coh-moh pweh-doh eer ah..)*
Do you know where I can find...?	¿Sabe dónde puedo encontrar...?	*(sah-beh dohn-deh pweh-doh ehn-kohn-trahr)*
Could you please tell me where I can find...?	¿Podría decirme dónde puedo encontrar...?	*(poh-dree-ah deh-seer-meh dohn-deh pweh-doh ehn-kohn-trahr?)*
May I ask you something?	¿Podría preguntarle algo?	*(poh-dree-ah preh-goon-tahr-leh ahl-goh)*
Excuse me, please!	¡Perdón, lo siento!	*(pehr-dohn loh see-entoh)*

CHAPTER SEVEN
TRANSPORTATION

By Train

Where's the nearest station?	¿Dónde está la estación más cerca?	*(dohn-deh ehs-tah lah ehs-tah-syohn mahs sehr-kah)*
When does the train from Buenos Aires arrive?	¿A qué hora llega el tren de Paris?	*(ah keh oh-rah yeh-gah ehl trehn deh Paris)*
When does the next train for Barcelona leave?	¿A qué hora sale el proximo tren a Sevilla?	*(ah keh oh-rah sah-leh prohk-see-moh trehn ah Seh-viyah)*
When does it arrive there?	¿A qué hora llegará allí?	*(ah keh oh-rah yeh-gahr-ah ahyee)*
Which platform does the train leave from?	¿El tren sale de que andén?	*(ehl trehn sah-leh deh keh ahn-dehn)*
Do I have to change?	¿Hace falta cambiar de tren?	*(ahseh fahl-tah kahm-byahr deh trehn)*
A single ticket for Barcelona, please.	Un billete sencillo para Barcelona, por favor.	*(oon bee-yeh-teh sehn-see-yoh pah-rah Bahr-seh-loh-nah, pohr fah-bohr)*
A return ticket for Santander, please.	Un billete de ida y vuelta para Santander, por favor.	*(oon bee-yeh-teh deh ee-dah ee bwehl-tah pah-rah Sahn-tahn-dehr, pohr fah-bohr)*

45

How long does the journey take?	¿Cuánto tiempo dure el viaje?	*(kwahn-toh tyehm-poh doo-reh ehl byah-heh)*
I would like to reserve a seat.	Quiero reservar una silla.	*(kyeh-roh rreh-sehr-bahr oo-nah see-yah)*
Is there a non-smoking seat?	¿Hay una plaza sin fumando?	*(ay oo-nah plas-ah sihn foo-mahn-doh)*
Does the train have a dining-car?	¿Hay coche-comedor en el tren?	*(ay koh-cheh coh-meh-dohr ehn ehl trehn)*
Has the 11:15 train already departed?	¿Ha ya el tren de once y cuarto llegado?	*(ah yah ehl trehn deh ohn-seh ee kwahr-toh yeh-gah-doh)*

My Plane

When does the next plane for New York leave?	¿A qué hora sale el próximo avión a Nueva York?	*(ah keh oh-rah sah-leh ehl prohk-see-moh ah-byohn ah Nuevah York)*
Is there a flight to New York this evening?	¿Hay vueltos a Nueva York esta tarde?	*(ay bwehl-toh ah Nueva York eh-stah tar-deh)*
I would like a seat in the non-smoking section.	Quiero una plaza en la sección non fumar.	*(kyeh-roh oo-nah plah-sah ehn lah sehk-syohn non foo-mahr)*
Is there a shuttle to the airport?	¿Hay trasladar al aeropuerto?	*(ay trahs-lah-dahr ahl ah-eh-roh-pwehr-toh)*

Is the plane due to leave on time?	¿El avión llegará puntualmente?	*(ehl ah-byohn yeh-gahr-ah poon-twahl-mehn-teh)*
I would like to change flights.	Quiero cambiar vuelta.	*(kyeh-roh kahm-byahr bwehl-tah)*
Can you confirm the time of arrival for the plane from ___?	¿Puede confirmar a qué hora llega el avión de ___?	*(pweh-deh kohm-feer-mahr ah keh ohr-rah yeh-gah ehl ah-byohn deh ___?)*
Can you confirm the time of departure for the plane to ___?	¿Puede confirmar a qué hora sale el avión para ___?	*(pweh-deh kohm-feer-mahr ah keh ohr-rah sah-leh ehl ah-byohn pah-rah ___?)*
Where is the duty free shop?	¿Dónde está la tienda libre de impuestos?	*(dohn-deh ehs-tah lah tyehn-dah deh eem-pwehs-toh)*
Where's the nearest bus stop?	¿Dónde está la parada de autobús más cerca?	*(dohn-deh ehs-tah lah pah-rah-dah deh ow-toh-boos mahs sehr-kah)*
Which bus do I take to get to the airport?	¿Qué autobús hace falta tomar para ir al aeropuerto?	*(keh ow-toh-boos ah-seh fahl-tah toh-mahr pah-rah eer ahl ah-eh-roh-pwehr-toh)*

By Bus

Can you get there by bus?	¿Se puede ir en autobús?	*(seh pweh-deh eer ehn ow-toh-boos?*
How frequent are the buses?	¿El autobús para Madrid sale de que pareda?	*(ehl ow-toh-boos pah-rah Madrid sah-leh deh keh pah-rehd?)*
How frequent are the buses?	¿Los autobuses salen con que frecuencia?	*(lohs ow-toh-boos-ehs sah-lehn cohn keh freh-kwehn-syah?)*
Is it direct?	¿Es directo?	*(ehs dee-rehk-toh)*
When is the first bus?	¿El primero autobús del día sale a que hora?	*(ehl pree-meh-roh ow-toh-boos dehl dee-ah sah-leh ah keh oh-rah)*
When is the last bus?	¿A qué hora ésta el último autobús del día?	*(ah keh oh-rah eh-stah ehl ool-tee-moh ow-toh-boos dehl dee-ah?)*
Have I missed the last bus?	¿He perdido el autobús?	*(eh pehr-dee-doh ehl ow-toh-boos?)*
Are there any free seats?	¿Hay plazas libres?	*(ay plas-ahs lee-breh)*
This seat is taken.	Esta plaza es ocupada.	*(eh-stah plas-ahs ehs oh-koo-pah-dah.)*
A book of tickets, please.	Un talonario de billetes, por favor.	*(oon tah-loh-nah-ryoh deh bee-yeh-teh, pohr fah-bohr)*
Do I get off here for the cinema?	¿Bajo del autobús allí para ir al cine?	*(bah-hoh dehl ow-toh-boos ah-yee pah-rah eer ahl see-neh)*

| Excuse me, this is my stop. | Perdón, pero allí está mi pareda. | *(pehr-dohn, peh-roh ah-yee eh-stah mee pah-rah-dah)* |

By Car

Where can I get a taxi?	¿Dónde puedo buscar un taxi?	*(dohn-deh pweh-doh boos-kahrr oon tahk-see)*
No entry.	Dirección prohibida.	*(dee-rehk-syohn proy-bee-doh)*
Follow this (small / large) road.	Seguid esta calle / carretera.	*(seh-geed eh-stah cah-yeh / kah-rreh-teh-rah)*
I have broken down.	Mi coche se he descompuesto.	*(meh koh-cheh seh eh dehs-kohm-pwehs-toh)*
I have run out of petrol/gas.	Me quedo sin gasolina.	*(meh keh-doh seen gah-soh-lee-nah)*
I have got a puncture.	Tengo un llanta pinchada.	*(tehn-goh oon yahn-tah peen-chah-dah)*
The battery is flat.	La batería está descargada.	*(lah bahk-teh-ryah eh-stah dehs-kahr-gah-doh)*
The engine won't start.	El motor no arranca.	*(ehl moh-tohr noh ah-rrahn-kahr)*
Five hundred pesos worth of unleaded, please.	Quinientos pesos de sin plomo.	*(kee-nyehn-tohs peh-sohs deh seen phloh-moh)*

Fill the tank up, please.	Llene el tanque con gasolina, por favor.	*(yeh-neh ehl tahn-keh cohn gah-soh-lee-nah, pohr fah-bohr)*
Please check the oil level.	Examinad el nivel del aceite, por favor.	*(ehk-sah-mee-nad ehl nee-behl dehl ah-sey-teh, pohr fah-bohr)*
Please check the water level.	Examinad el nivel del agua, por favor.	*(ehk-sah-mee-nad ehl nee-behl dehl ah-gwah, pohr fah-bohr)*
Please check the tyres.	Examinad los neumáticos, por favor.	*(ehk-sah-mee-nad lohs neyoo-mah-tee-koh, pohr fah-bohr)*
Please check the battery.	Examinad la batería, por favor.	*(ehk-sah-mee-nad lah bah-teh-ree-ah, pohr fah-bohr)*
Please switch the engine off.	Encienda el motor, por favor.	*(ehn-sehn-dehr ehl moh-tohr, pohr fah-bohr)*

CHAPTER EIGHT
DESCRIBING THINGS AND PEOPLE

Starting a Sentence

You are...(permanent)	Eres...	*(eh-rehs)*
You are... (temporary)	Estas...	*(ehs-tahs)*
You are very...	Eres muy...	*(eh-rehs mwee...)*
You are very...	Estas muy...	*(ehs-tahs mwee...)*
The man (with)...	El hombre (con)...	*(ehl ohm-breh (cohn))*
The woman (with)...	La mujer (con)...	*(lah moo-hehr (cohn))*

Physical Descriptors

attractive	atractivo	*(ah-trahk-tee-boh)*
average	promedio	*(proh-meh-dyoh)*
blond	rubio	*(rroo-byoh)*
fat	gordo	*(gohr-doh)*
lovely	lindo	*(leen-doh)*
plump	rechoncho	*(rreh-chohn-choh)*
pretty	bonita	*(boh-nee-toh)*
short	bajo	*(bah-hoh)*
slim	delgado	*(dehl-gah-doh)*

small	pequeño	*(peh-keh-nyoh)*
strong	fuerte	*(fwehr-teh)*
tall	alto	*(ahl-toh)*
thin	flaco	*(flah-koh)*
ugly	feo	*(feh-oh)*
weak	débil	*(deh-beel)*
bald	calvo	*(kahl-boh)*
fair	rubio	*(rroo-byoh)*
brown hair	cabello castaño	*(kah-beh-yoh kahs-tah-nyoh)*
curly hair	cabello rizado	*(kah-beh-yoh rree-sah-doh)*
dark hair	cabello oscuro	*(kah-beh-yoh ohs-koo-roh)*
grey hair	cabello canoso	*(kah-beh-yoh kah-noh-soh)*
handsome	guapo	*(gwah-poh)*
lame	cojo	*(koh-hoh)*
light hair	cabello claro	*(kah-beh-yoh klah-roh)*
long hair	cabello largo	*(kah-beh-yoh lahr-goh)*
maimed	mutilado	*(moo-tee-lah-doh)*
muscular	musculoso	*(moos-koo-loh-soh)*
one-eyed	tuerto	*(twehr-toh)*
pale	pálido	*(pah-lee-doh)*
plain	poco atractivo	*(poh-coh ah-trahk-tee-boh)*
redhead	pelirrojo	*(peh-lee-rroh-hoh)*
scruffy	desaliñado	*(dehs-ah-lee-nyah-doh)*
short hair	cabello corto	*(kah-beh-yoh kohr-toh)*

slender	esbelto	*(ehs-behl-toh)*
squint	bizco	*(bees-koh)*
stout	corpulento	*(kohr-poo-lehn-toh)*
straight hair	cabello lacio	*(kah-beh-yoh lah-syoh)*
tanned	bronceado	*(brohn-seh-ah-doh)*
tiny	pequeño	*(peh-keh-nyoh)*
well-built	fornido	*(fohr-nee-doh)*
old	viejo	*(byeh-hoh)*
young	joven	*(hoh-behn)*
obese	obeso	*(oh-beh-soh)*
braid	trenza	*(trehn-sah)*
ponytail	cola	*(koh-lah)*
beard	barba	*(bahr-bah)*
freckle	peca	*(peh-kah)*
mole	lunar	*(loo-nahr)*
moustache	bigote	*(bee-goh-teh)*
scar	cicatriz	*(see-kah-trees)*
sideburns	patillas	*(pah-tee-yah)*
tattoo	tatuaje	*(tah-twah-heh)*
wart	verruga	*(beh-rroo-gah)*
wrinkle	arruga	*(ah-rroo-gah)*
elegant	elegante	*(eh-leh-gahn-teh)*

Describing Things

sour	ácido	*(ah-see-doh)*
stinky	apestoso	*(ah-pehs-toh-soh)*
shiny	brillante	*(bree-yahn-teh)*

noisy	bullicioso	*(boo-yee-syoh-soh)*
hot	caliente	*(kah-lyehn-teh)*
colorful	colorido	*(koh-loh-ree-doh)*
sweet	dulce	*(dool-seh)*
hard	duro	*(doo-roh)*
cold	frío	*(free-oh)*
odorless	inodoro	*(ee-noh-doh-roh)*
bright	luminoso	*(loo-mee-noh-soh)*
musical	musical	*(moo-see-kahl)*
smelly	oloroso	*(oh-loh-roh-soh)*
scented	perfumado	*(pehr-foo-mah-doh)*
spicy	picante	*(pee-kahn-teh)*
loud	ruidoso	*(rrwee-doh-soh)*
salty	salado	*(sah-lah-doh)*
silent	silencioso	*(see-lehn-syoh-soh)*
soft	suave	*(swah-beh)*
transparent	transparente	*(trahns-pah-rehn-teh)*

Parts of the Body

Arm	el brazo	*(brrah-soh)*
Back	la espalda	*(ehs-pahl-dah)*
Brain	el cerebro	*(seh-reh-broh)*
Breast, chest	el pecho	*(peh-choh)*
Buttocks	las nalgas	*(nahl-gah)*
Calf	la pantorrilla	*(pahn-toh-rree-yah)*
Ear	el oído	*(oh-ee-doh)*
Elbow	el codo	*(koh-doh)*

Eye	el ojo	*(oh-hoh)*
Finger	el dedo	*(deh-doh)*
Foot	el pie	*(pyeh)*
Hair	el pelo	*(peh-loh)*
Hand	la mano	*(mah-noh)*
Head	la cabeza	*(kah-beh-sah)*
Heart	el corazón	*(koh-rah-sohn)*
Hip	la cadera	*(kah-deh-rah)*
Intestine	el intestino	*(een-tehs-tee-noh)*
Knee	la rodilla	*(rroh-dee-yah)*
Leg	la pierna	*pyehr-nah)*
Liver	el hígado	*(ee-gah-doh)*
Mouth	la boca	*(boh-kah)*
Muscle	el músculo	*(moos-koo-loh)*
Neck	el cuello	*(kweh-yoh)*
Nose	la nariz	*(nah-rees)*
Shoulder	el hombro	*(ohm-broh)*
Skin	la piel	*(pyehl)*
Stomach (abdomen)	el vientre	*(byehn-treh)*
Stomach (internal organ)	el estómago	*(ehs-toh-mah-goh)*
Thigh	el muslo	*(moos-loh)*
Throat	la garganta	*(gahr-gahn-tah)*
Toe	el dedo del pie	*(deh-doh dehl pyeh)*
Tongue	la lengua	*(lehng-gwah)*
Tooth	el diente	*(dyehn-teh)*

CHAPTER NINE
ACCOMMODATIONS AND HOTELS

Checking In

Is there a car park?	¿Hay aparcamiento?	*(ay ah-pahr-kah-myehn-toh)*
Is there a restaurant in the hotel?	¿Hay restaurante en el hotel?	*(ay rrehs-tow-rahn-teh ehn ehl oh-tehl)*
Is there a lift/elevator?	¿Hay ascensor en el hotel?	*(ay ah-sehn-sohr ehn ehl oh-tehl)*
Is there a shop on the camp site?	¿Hay tiendas en el acampada?	*(ay tyehn-dahs ehn ehl kahmp-ihng)*
Is there an electric connection for our caravan?	¿Hay tomas de corriente eléctrica para el remolque tienda?	*(ay toh-mahs deh koh-rryehn-teh eh-lehk-trih-kah pah-rah ehl rreh-mohl-keh tyehn-dahs)*
Is there a swimming pool?	¿Hay una piscina?	*(ay oo-nah pee-see-nah)*
Is there another hotel near here?	¿Hay otro hotel cerca de aquí?	*(ay oh-troh oh-tehl sehr-kah deh ah-kee)*
How much is a single / double room per night?	¿Cuánto cuesta un habitación individual / doble por noche?	*(kwahn-toh kwehs-tah oohn ah-bee-tah-syohn ihn-dih-vihj-u-uhl / doh-bleh pohr noh-cheh)*

What is the price?	¿Cuánto cuesta?	*(kwahn-toh kwehs-tah)*
How much does it cost per day?	¿Cuál es el precio por día?	*(kwahl ehs ehl preh-syoh dee-ah)*
Is breakfast included?	¿Incluye desayuno?	*(eeng-klwyeh dehs-ah-yoo-noh)*
What time does the hotel close in the evenings?	¿A qué hora cierran la puerta de entrada?	*(ah keh oh-rah see-ehrr-ahn lah pweh-rtah deh ehn-trah-dah)*
When is dinner served?	¿A qué hora es la cena?	*(ah keh oh-rah ehs lah seh-nah)*
Can somebody please bring my cases up.	¿Podría preguntar a alguien a llevar mis maletas a mi habitación?	*(poh-drry-ah preh-goon-tahr ah ahl-gyehn ah yeh-bahr mihs mah-leh-tah ah mee ah-bee-tah-syohn)*
Do you have any rooms available (for the 5th June)?	¿Quedan habitaciones libres (para el cinco de junio)?	*(keh-dahn ah-bee-tah-syohnes lee-brehys (pah-rah ehl seeng-koh deh hoo-lyoh)*
Where is the reception, please?	¿Dónde está la recepción por favor?	*(dohn-deh eh-stah lah rreh-sehp-syohn, pohr fah-bohr)*
Where is the television room?	¿Dónde está la habitación de televisor?	*(dohn-deh eh-stah lah ah-bee-tah-syohn deh teh-leh-bee-sohr)*
Where is the games room?	¿Dónde está la habitación de juegos?	*(dohn-deh ehs-tah lah ah-bee-tah-syohn deh hweh-gohs)*
Where's the toilet/shower block?	¿Dónde están los servicios/ las duchas?	*(dohn-deh ehs-tahn lohs sehr-bee-syoh / lahs doo-chahs)*

Where are the trash cans?	¿Dónde están los cubos de basura?	*(dohn-deh ehs-tahn lohs koo-boh deh bah-sur-ah)*
Do you have room for a tent?	¿Tiene un sitio para una tienda?	*(tyeh-neh oon see-tyoh pah-rah oo-nah tyehn-dah)*
Does the hotel have Internet access?	¿Tiene el hotel acceso a Internet?	*(tyeh-neh ehl oh-tehl ahk-seh-soh ah een-tehr-neht)*
Do you have any rooms available for tonight?	¿Tiene alguna habitación por este noche?	*(tyeh-nehs ahl-goon-ah ah-bee-tah-syohn pohr ehs-teh noh-cheh)*
I'm sorry, we are full.	Estoy arrepentido pero estamos completos.	*(ehs-toy ah-rreh-pehn-tee-doh peh-roh eh-stah-mos kohm-pleh-toh)*
We would like to stay for three nights.	Queremos quedarnos hasta el próximo sábado.	*(kyeh-reh-mos keh-dahr-nos ahs-tah ehl prohk-see-moh sah-bah-doh)*
May I have towels for room 2 please.	¿Puedo tener tres toallas para la habitación dos?	*(pweh-doh tehn-ehr toh-ah-yahs pah-rah lah ah-bee-tah-syohn dohs)*
I would like two single rooms and a double room as well.	Quiero dos habitaciones individuales.	*(kyeh-roh dohs ah-bee-tah-syohnes een-dee-bee-dwah-lehs)*
I would like a room with a shower.	Quiero un habitación con una ducha.	*(kyeh-roh oon ah-bee-tah-syon cohn oo-nah doo-chah)*

During Your Stay

Can I flush the toilet paper?	¿Puedo lavar el papel higiénico?	*(pweh-doh lah-bahr ehl pah-pehl ee-hyeh-nee-koh)*
Can I drink the tap water?	¿Puedo beber el agua del grifo?	*(pweh-doh beh-ber ehl agh-wah dehl gree-foh)*
Can you wash and iron my shirt?	¿Puedes lavar y planchar mi camisa?	*(pweh-dehs lah-bahr ee plahn-chahr mee kah-mee-sah)*
Can you wake me at eight o'clock?	¿Me puede despertar a las ocho horas?	*(meh pweh-deh dehs-pehr-tahr ah lahs oh-choh oh-rahs)*
Am I speaking to the bar?	¿Hablo con el bar?	*(Ah-bloh cohn ehl bar)*
What time do you serve breakfast / lunch / dinner?	¿A que hora comienza el servicio de desayunos / comidas / cenas?	*(Ah keh oh-rah koh-mehn-sahr ehl sehr-bee-syoh deh dehs-ah-yoo-nohs / koh-mee-dah / seh-nahr)*
Can you give me the key to room 206?	¿Puede darme la llave de la habitación 206?	*(pweh-deh dahr-meh lah yah-beh deh lah ah-bee-tah-syohn 206)*
Do you have an outlet adaptor?	¿Tiene un adaptador de salida?	*(tyeh-neh oon ah-dahp-tah-dohr deh sah-lee-dah)*

Complaints

There is no toilet paper in my room.	No hay papel higiénico en mi habitación.	*(noh ay pah-pehl ee-hyeh-nee-koh ehn mee ah-bee-tah-syohn)*

| I have a problem. | Tengo una problema. | *(tehn-goh oo-nah proh-bleh-mah)* |
| I'm sorry I don't understand. Could you speak more slowly please? | ¿Me puede hablar más despacio por favor? | *(meh pweh-deh ah-blahr mahs dehs-pah-syoh pohr fah-bohr)* |

Checking Out

Could you get my bill ready please?	¿Me puede preparar la cuenta por favor?	*(meh pweh-deh preh-pahr-ahr lah kwehn-tah pohr fah-bohr)*
We'll be leaving tomorrow morning.	Nos vamos mañana por la mañana.	*(nohs vah-mohs mah-nyah-nah pohr lah mah-nyah-nah)*
I'll be leaving tomorrow afternoon / night.	Me voy mañana por la tarde / noche.	*(meh boy mah-nyah-nah pohr lah tahr-deh / noh-cheh)*
Do you take credit cards?	¿Aceptan tarjetas de crédito?	*(ah-sehp-tahn tahr-heh-tah deh kreh-dee-toh)*

Important Vocabulary

Do not disturb	No molestar	*(noh moh-lehs-tahr)*
Fire escape	Escalera de incendios	*(ehs-kah-leh-rah deh een-sehn-dyoh)*
Fire exit	Salida de incendios	*(sah-lee-dah deh een-sehn-dyoh)*

Toilet paper	el papel higiénico	*(ehl pah-pehl ee-hyeh-nee-koh)*
Throw it in the toilet or trash can?	¿Tirarlo al inodoro o a la basura?	*(tee-rahr-loh ahl ee-noh-doh-roh oh ah lah bah-soo-rah)*
Can I drink the tap water?	¿Puedo beber el agua del grifo?	*(pweh-doh beh-behr ehl ah-gwah dehl gree-foh)*
Bed bugs!	¡Chinches!	*(cheen-chehs)*
I lost my key	Perdí mi llave	*(pehr-dy mee yah-beh)*
___ is not working	___ no funciona	*(___, noh foon-syoh-nah)*
Laundry	la ropa sucia	*(rroh-pah soo-syah)*
per night	Por noche	*(pohr noh-cheh)*
per person	Por persona	*(pohr pehr-soh-nah)*
swimming pool	Piscina	*(pee-see-nah)*
bed	Cama	*(kah-mah)*
cheap	Barato/a	*(bah-rah-toh)*
blanket	Manta	*(mahn-tah)*
air conditioning	Aire Acondicionado	*(ay-reh ah-kohn-dee-syoh-nah-doh)*
key	Llave	*(yah-beh)*
safe	La caja de seguridad	*(lah kah-hah deh seh-goo-ree-dahd)*

CHAPTER TEN
SPECIAL OCCASIONS

Questions and Instructions

Where is the party going to be?	¿Dónde está la fiesta?	*(dohn-deh ehs-tah lah fyehs-tah)*
Can you please give me directions to the party?	¿Puedes darme direcciones a la fiesta, por favor?	*(pweh-dehs dahr-meh dee-rehk-syohn ah lah fyehs-tah, pohr fah-bor)*
Whose house is the party going to be at?	¿En la casa de quien van a poner la fiesta?	*(ehn lah cah-sah deh kyehn vahn ah poh-nehr lah fyehs-tah)*
About what time does the party begin?	¿Como a que horas empieza la fiesta?	*(coh-moh ah keh ohr-ahs ehm-pee-ehsah lah fyehs-tah)*
Is Peter coming to the party?	¿Va a venir Pedro a la fiesta?	*(vah ah beh-neer Pedro ah lah fyehs-tah)*
Do you want to dance with me?	¿Quieres bailar conmigo?	*(kyeh-rehs bay-lahr kohn-mee-goh)*
The party starts at 8 o'clock.	La fiesta empieza a las ocho.	*(lah fyehs-tah ehm-py-ehzah ah lah oh-choh)*
Bring your own beer.	Traiga tu propia cerveza.	*(trahy-gah too proh-py-nah sehr-vehs-ah)*

The party is to celebrate Paul's birthday.	La fiesta es para celebrar el cumpleaños de Pablo.	*(lah fyesh-stah ehs pah-rah seh-leh-brahr ehl koom-pleh-ah-nyohs deh Pablo)*
There will be about 30 people at the party.	Van a estar como 30 personas en la fiesta.	*(bahn ah ehs-tahr coh-moh (30) pehr-soh-nah ehn lah fyehs-tah)*
Can you please give me a ride to the party?	¿Puedes darme un rite a la fiesta?	*(pweh-dehs dahr-meh oon rayt ah lah fyehs-tah)*

Special Phrases

Merry/Happy Christmas	Feliz Navidad	*(feh-lees nah-bee-dahd)*
Happy Holidays	Felices Fiestas	*(feh-lee-sehs fyehs-tahs)*
Happy New Year	Próspero Año Nuevo	*(prohs-peh-roh ah-nyoh nweh-boh)*

CHAPTER ELEVEN
QUICK ABOUT YOU

Where do you work?	¿Donde trabajas?	*(dohn-deh trah-bah-hahs)*
I work at a restaurant.	Trabajo en un restaurante.	*(trah-bah-hoh ehn oon rrehs-tow-rahn-teh)*
What are your hobbies?	¿Cuáles son tus aficiones?	*(kwahl-ehs sohn toos ah-fee-syoh-nahr)*
I like to read books and watch movies.	Me gusta leer libros y ver películas.	*(meh gooh-stah leh-ehr lee-brohs ee vehr peh-lee-koo-lahs)*
Where are you from?	¿De donde eres?	*(deh dohn-deh eh-rehs)*
I'm from ___.	Soy de ___.	*(soy deh ___)*
What's your favorite movie?	¿Cuál es tu película favorita?	*(kwahl ehs too peh-lee-koo-lah fah-boh-ree-toh)*
I love ___.	Me encanta ___.	*(meh ehn-kahn-tah)*
How long have you been learning Spanish?	¿Desde cuándo aprendes español?	*(dehs-deh kwahn-doh ah-prehn-dehs ehs-pah-nyohl)*
I've been learning Spanish for 3 months.	Aprendo español desde hace ___ meses.	*(ah-prehn-doh ehs-pah-nyohl dehs-deh ah-seh ___ meh-sehs)*
What is your favourite color?	¿Cuál es tu color favorito?	*(kwahl ehs too coh-lohr fah-boh-ree-toh)*

I like green.	Me gusta el verde.	*(meh gooh-stah ehl vehr-deh)*
Do you speak other languages?	¿Hablas otros idiomas?	*(ah-blahs oh-troh ee-dyoh-mah)*
Yes, I speak English and French.	Sí, hablo inglés y francés.	*(see, ah-bloh eeng-glehs ee frahn-sehs)*

CHAPTER TWELVE
BUYING FOOD AND HOME COOKING

Common Conversation

How much is a kilo of strawberries?	¿A cuánto está el kilo de fresas?	*(ah kwahn-toh ehs-tah ehl kih-loh deh freh-sahs)*
$2.50—not a penny more.	A dos cincuenta nada más.	*(Ah dohs seeng-kwehn-tah nah-dah mahs)*
Anything else?	¿Alguna otra cosa más?	*(ahl-goon-ah oh-trah coh-sah mahs)*
How much is everything?	¿Cuánto es todo?	*(kwahn-toh ehs toh-doh)*
Yes, a lettuce and a kilo of tomatoes	Sí, una lechuga y un kilo de tomates.	*(see, oo-nah leh-choo-gah ee oon kee-loh deh toh-mah-tehs)*
I'll give you a bit of parsley too.	Te pongo un poco de perejil también.	*(teh pohn-goh oon poh-coh deh peh-reh-heel tahm-byehn)*
They are $3.25.	Son tres con veinticinco.	*(sohn trehs cohn beyn-tee-seeng-koh)*
Can I have __ kilograms of __?	Puedo tener __ kilo de __?	*(pweh-doh teh-nehr __ kee-loh deh ___)*

Fruit

fruit	la fruta	*(froo-tah)*
strawberry	la fresa	*(freh-sah)*
lemon	el limón	*(lee-mohn)*
peach	el melocotón (Sp.) el durazno (L. America)	*(meh-loh-koh-tohn)* *(doo-rahs-noh)*
orange	la naranja	*(nah-rahng-hah)*
apple	la manzana	*(mahn-sah-nah)*
pear	la pera	*(peh-rah)*
cherry	la cereza	*(seh-reh-sah)*
raspberry	la frambuesa	*(frahm-bweh-sah)*
avocado	el aguacate	*(ah-gwah-kah-teh)*
tomato	el tomate	*(toh-mah-teh)*
banana	el plátano	*(plah-tah-noh)*
melon	el melón	*(meh-lohn)*

Vegetables

vegetables and pulses	las legumbres	*(leh-goom-breh)*
(green) vegetable	la verdura	*(behr-doo-rah)*
vegetable	la hortaliza	*(ohr-tah-lee-sah)*
onion	la cebolla	*(seh-boh-yah)*
lettuce	la lechuga	*(leh-choo-gah)*
carrot	la zanahoria	*(sah-nah-oh-ryah)*
aubergine/eggplant	la berenjena	*(beh-rehng-heh-nah)*

cucumber	el pepino	*(peh-pee-noh)*
potato	la papa	*(pah-pah)*
leek	el puerro	*(pweh-rroh)*
green beans	las judía verde	*(hoo-dee-ah behr-deh)*
spinach	las espinacas	*(ehs-pee-nah-kah)*

Herbs and Spices

parsley	el perejil	*(peh-reh-heel)*
rosemary	el romero	*(rroh-meh-rroh)*
thyme	el tomillo	*(toh-mee-yoh)*
mint	la menta	*(mehn-tah)*
paprika	el pimentón	*(pee-mehn-tohn)*
garlic	el ajo	*(ah-hoh)*

Meat

meat (beef)	la carne	*(kahr-neh)*
salami	el salchichón	*(sahl-chee-chohn)*
pork	el cerdo	*(sehr-doh)*
chicken	el pollo	*(poh-yoh)*
lamb	el cordero	*(kohr-deh-roh)*
veal	la ternera	*(tehr-neh-rah)*

Ordering

Give me	póngame ...	*(pohn-gah-meh...)*
Could you give me ..., please?	¿Me pone ..., por favor?	*(meh poh-neh..., pohr fah-bohr)*
How much does ... cost?	¿Cuánto cuesta ...?	*(kwahn-toh kwehs-tah...?)*
How much is it?	¿Cuánto es?	*(kwahn-toh ehs...?)*
Two fifty	dos (dolares con) cincuenta (céntimos) $2.50	*(dohs seeng-kwehn-tah)*

Amounts

1kg	un kilo	*(kee-loh)*
500g	medio kilo	*(meh-dyoh kee-loh)*
250g	un cuarto de kilo	*(kwahr-toh deh kee-loh)*
100g	cien gramos	*(syehn grah-moh)*
a dozen	una docena	*(oo-nah doh-seh-nah)*
half a dozen	media docena	*(meh-dyah doh-seh-nah)*
bag	una bolsa	*(oo-nah bohl-sah)*
packet	un paquete	*(pah-keh-teh)*

Other things to say...

Is this fresh / ripe / organic?	¿Es fresco?	*(ehs frehs-koh)*
free-range egg	el huevo campero	*(weh-boh kahm-peh-roh)*
bread	el pan	*(pahn)*
cheese	el queso	*(keh-soh)*
fish	el pescado	*(pehs-kah-doh)*
Where is the baker / butcher / fishmonger?	¿Donde está la panadería / la carnicería / la pescadería?	*(dohn-deh ehs-tah lah pah-nah-deh-ree-ah/ lah kahr-nee-seh-ree-ah/ lah pehs-kah-deh-ree-ah)*
rotten	podrido	*(poh-dree-doh)*

CHAPTER THIRTEEN
RESTAURANTS

Questions You'll Hear

Would you like something to eat?	¿Quieres algo a comer?	*(kyeh-rehs al-goh ah coh-mehr)*
Would you like something to drink?	¿Quieres algo a beber?	*(kyeh-rehs al-goh ah beh-behr)*
What would you like to eat?	¿Qué quieres comer?	*(keh kyeh-rehs coh-mehr)*
What would you like to drink?	¿Que quieres beber?	*(keh kyeh-rehs behber)*
What types of sandwiches do you have?	¿Que tipo de sándwich tienes?	*(keh tee-poh deh sahnd-wihch tyeh-nehs)*
What flavors do you have?	¿Que sabores de helados tienes?	*(keh sah-bohr-ehs deh eh-lah-dohs tyeh-nehs)*
What do you recommend?	¿Que nos recomienda?	*(keh nohs rreh-koh-mehn-dah)*

Restaurants and Cafes

Do you have a table for ___?	¿Tienes una mesa para ___ personas?	*(tyeh-nehs oo-nah meh-sah par-ah ___ pehr-soh-nahs)*
I would like a table near the window.	Quisiera una mesa a lado de la ventana.	*(kee-syeh-rah oo-nah meh-sah ah lah-doh lah behn-tah-nah)*

I have a table reserved in the name Johnson.	Tengo una reserva para ___.	*(tehn-goh oo-nah rreh-sehr-bah pah-rah ___)*
I would like to see the menu, please.	Quiero ver el menú, por favor.	*(kyeh-roh vehr ehl meh-noo pohr fah-bohr)*
I would like to order now.	Quiero pedir una cena ahora.	*(kyeh-roh peh-deer oo-nah seh-nah ah-oh-rah)*
To start, I would like the prawns / shrimps.	De primero quiero los gambas / camarones.	*(deh pree-meh-roh kyeh-roh lohs gahm-bahs / kahm-ruhn)*
For the main course, I would like steak.	Como plato principal quiero un bistec.	*(coh-moh plah-toh preen-see-pahl kyeh-roh oon bees-tehk)*
For dessert, I'll have apple tart.	De postre quiero flan.	*(deh pohstreh kyeh-roh flahn)*
To drink, I would like some white wine.	Para beber, quiero el vino blanco.	*(Pah-rah beh-ber, kyeh-roh ehl vee-noh blahn-koh)*
That's not what I ordered.	Esto no es lo que he pedido.	*(ehs-toh noh ehs loh keh eh peh-dee-doh)*
Waiter!	Camarero!	*(kah-mah-reh-roh)*
Could I have the bill, please.	La cuenta, por favor.	*(lah kwehn-tah, pohr fah-bohr)*
Will you bring me the bill?	¿Me traes la cuenta?	*(meh trah-ehs lah kwehn-tah)*
Is service included?	¿La propina está incluida?	*(lah proh-pee-nah ehs eeng-klwee-dah)*
I'm not ready yet.	Todavía no estoy listo.	*(toh-dah-bee-ah noh ehs-toy lees-toh)*

I need more time.	Necesito más tiempo .	*(neh-seh-see-tahr mahs tyehm-poh)*
Will you bring me another fork?	¿Me traes otro tenedor?	*(meh trah-ehes oh-troh teh-neh-dohr)*
Will you bring me more bread?	¿Me traes más pan?	*(meh trah-ehes mahs pahn)*
What do you recommend?	¿Qué me recomienda?	*(keh meh rreh-koh-mehn-dee-ah)*
Can we pay separately?	¿Podemos pagar por separado?	*(poh-dehmohs pah-gahr pohr seh-pah-rah-doh)*
Thank you. Keep the change.	Gracias. Quédese el cambio	*(grah-syahs. keh-deeh-seh ehl kahm-byoh)*
Is it spicy?	¿Es picante?	*(ehs pee-kahn-teh)*
Where is the bathroom?	¿Dónde está el baño?	*(dohn-deh ehs-tah ehl ban-yoh)*

Allergy Explanations

I'm allergic to ___ / My child is allergic to ___.	Soy alérgico(a) a _____ / Mi niño(a) es alérgico(a) a _____.	*(Soy ah-lehr-hee-koh(ah) ah _____ / Mee nee-nyoh ehs ah-lehr-hee-koh(ah ___)*
milk	la leche	*(leh-cheh)*
eggs	los huevos	*(weh-boh)*
peanut	los cacahuates	*(kah-kah-wah-teh)*
nuts	nueces	*(nwehs)*
fish	pescado	*(pehs-kah-doh)*
shellfish	mariscos	*(mah-rees-koh)*
wheat	trigo	*(tree-goh)*

soy	soya	*(soh-yah)*
gluten	gluten	*(glu-dihn)*
almonds	almendras	*(ahl-mehn-drah)*

Menu Vocabulary

an appetizer	una entrada	*(oo-nah en-tra-da)*
a main dish	un plato principal	*(oon pla-toh prin-si-pal)*
a dessert	un postre	*(oon pos-tray)*
a drink	una bebida	*(oo-nah beh-bee-da)*
soup	una sopa	*(oo-nah soh-pah)*
salad	una ensalada	*(oo-nah en-sa-la-da)*
chicken	el pollo	*(el poy-oh)*
meat (beef)	la carne	*(la car-nay)*
water	una agua	*(oo-nah ag-wa)*
red wine	un vino tinto / blanco	*(oon vee-noh tin-toh / blan-koh)*
beer	una cerveza	*(oo-nah ser-vay-sa)*
coffee	un café	*(oon ka-fay)*

Complaints

I'd like to complain about...	Quisiera quejarme de...	*(kee-syeh-rah keh-har-meh deh...)*
I'm having trouble with...	Estoy teniendo problemas con...	*(eh-stoy teh-nyen-doh proh-bleh-mahs cohn...)*
It's hot.	Está caluroso	*(ehs-tah kah-loo-roh-soh)*

It's cold.	Está frío	*(ehs-tah free-yoh)*
It's too expensive.	Es muy caro.	*(ehs mwee kah-roh)*
It's noisy.	Hay mucho ruido.	*(hay moo-choh rrwee-doh)*
I'm starving.	Me estoy muriendo de hambre.	*(meh eh-stoy moh-ree-en-doh deh ahm-breh*
The Wi-Fi here is too slow.	El Wi-Fi aquí es demasiado lento.	*(ehl Wee-Fee ah-kee ehs deh-mah-syah-doh lehn-toh)*
That's not what I ordered.	Esto no es lo que he pedido.	*(ehs-toh noh ehs loh keh eh peh-dee-doh)*
I think there is a mistake in the bill.	Pienso que haya un error en la cuenta.	*(pyehn-soh keh ayah oon eh-rrohr ehn lah kwehn-tah)*

Ordering a Steak

Rare	muy jugoso	*(mwee hoo-goh-soh)*
Medium rare	jugosa	*(hoo-goh-sah)*
Medium	a punto	*(ah poon-toh)*
Medium well	cocida	*(koh-see-doh)*

Well done	bien cocida	*(byehn koh-see-doh)*

CHAPTER FOURTEEN
SHOPPING

Opening and Questions

Open at 10	Abierto a las 10	*(ah-byehr-toh ah lahs dyehs)*
Are there ...? Do you have ...?	¿Hay ...?	*(ay...)*
Cash register; cashier	La caja; el cajero, la cajera	*(lah kah-hah; ehl kah-heroh, lah kah-herah)*
Thank you, thank you very much	Gracias, muchas gracias, mil gracias	*(grah-syahs, moo-chas grah-syahs, meel grah-syahs)*
I don't want it.	No lo/la/los/las quiero.	*(noh loh/lah/lohs/lahs kyeh-roh)*
I want..., please.	Quiero..., por favor.	*(kyeh-roh..., pohr fah-bohr)*
I would like to try it (on), please.	Quisiera probarlo, por favor.	*(kee-syeh-rah proh-bahr-loh. pohr fah-bohr)*
I would like..., please.	Quisiera..., por favor.	*(kee-syeh-rah..., pohr fah-bohr)*
I'll think about it.	Voy a pensarlo.	*(boy ah pehn-sahr-loh)*
Please	Por favor	*(pohr fah-bohr)*
I'm only looking.	Sólo quería mirar.	*(soh-loh (kyeh-ree-ah meer-ahr)*

| I'll come back soon. I'll come back later. | Vuelvo pronto. Vuelvo más tarde. | *(buehl-boh prohn-toh. buehl-boh mahs tahr-deh)* |

More Conversations

Cheap	Barato	*(bah-rah-toh)*
Expensive	Caro, cara	*(kah-roh/rah)*
To buy	Comprar	*(kohm-prahr)*
What is the exchange rate?	¿Cuál es el cambio?	*(kwahl ehs ehl cahm-bee-oh)*
How much does it cost? How much do they cost?	¿Cuánto cuesta? ¿Cuánto cuestan?	*(kwahn-toh kwehs-tah; kwahn-toh kwehs-tahn)*
How much is it worth? How much are they worth?	¿Cuánto vale? ¿Cuánto valen?	*(kwahn-toh bah-leh;kwahn-toh bah-lehn)*
How much (in dollars)? How much (in pesos)? How much (in euros)?	¿Cuantos dólares? ¿Cuantos pesos? ¿Cuántos euros?	*(kwahn-tohs doh-lahrs; kwahn-tohs peh-sohs; kwahn-tohs yur-ohs)*
Where can I buy ...?	¿Dónde puedo comprar ...?	*(dohn-deh pweh-doh kohm-prahr ...)*
Discount	Descuento	*(dehs-kwehn-toh)*
On sale	En oferta, en oferta especial	*(ehn oh-fehr-tah, ehn oh-fehr-tah ehs-pah-syahl)*
Price reduction	Rebaja	*(rreh-bah-hah)*

On sale, at a discount	De rebajas	*(deh rreh-bah-hah)*
For sale, on sale	En venta, a la venta	*(ehn behn-tah, ah lah behn-tah))*
Credit card; Are credit cards accepted?	Tarjeta de crédito; ¿Se aceptan tarjetas de crédito?	*(tahr-heh-tah deh kreh-dee-toh; seh ah-sehp-tahn tahr-heh-tahs deh kreh-dee-toh)*
To sell, seller	Vender, vendedor	*(behn-dehr, behn-dehr-dohr)*
Do you have ... in other colors? Do you have ... in other sizes?	¿Hay ... en otros colores? ¿Hay ... en otras tallas?	*(ay... ehn oh-trohs koh-lohrs; ay... ehn oh-trah tah-yahr)*
Good quality	De buena calidad	*(deh bweh-nah kah-lee-dahd)*
Poor quality	De mala calidad	*(deh mah-lah kah-lee-dahd)*
Small	Pequeño, pequeña	*(peh-keh-nyoh, peh-keh-nyah)*
Medium (in size)	Mediano, mediana	*(meh-dyah-noh, meh-dyah-nah)*
Large	Grande	*(grahn-deh)*
They're very pretty.	Son muy bonitos. Son muy bonitas.	*(sohn mwee boh-nee-tohs, sohn mwee boh-nee-tahs)*

CHAPTER FIFTEEN
SOCIALIZING

Introducing Yourself

"What do you like to do?"	¿Qué te gusta hacer?	*(keh teh goo-stah ah-sehr)*
"My favorite pastime is…"	Mi pasatiempo favorito es…	*(mee pah-sah-tyehm-poh fah-boh-ree-toh ehs…)*
"What are your hobbies?"	¿Cuáles son tus pasatiempos?	*(kwahl-ehs sohn toohs pah-sah-tyehm-poh)*
"What do you do in your free time?"	¿Qué haces en tu tiempo libre?	*(keh ah-sehs ehn too tyehm-poh lee-breh)*
"I like / I don't like…"	Me gusta / No me gusta…	*(meh goo-stah / noh meh goo-stah)*
"I love…"	Me encanta…	*(meh ehng-kahn-tah…)*
"Do you like to read?"	¿Qué te gusta leer?	*(keh teh goo-stah leh-ehr)*
"What music do you like?"	¿Que música te gusta?	*(keh moo-see-kah teh goo-stah)*
"My favourite is…"	Mi favorito es…	*(mee fah-boh-ree-toh ehs…)*
"I like going to…"	Me gusta ir…	*(meh goo-stah eehr…)*
"What's your job?"	¿En qué trabajas?	*(ehn keh trah-bah-hahr)*
"Do you like	¿Te gusta tu	*(teh goo-stah too trah-bah-*

your job?"	trabajo?	*hoh)*
"I work at…"	Trabajo en…	*(trah-bah-hoh ehn…)*

Conversation Starters

Where are you from?	¿De dónde eres?	*(deh dohn-deh eh-rehs)*
What do you do for a living?	¿A qué te dedicas?	*(ah keh teh deh-dee-kahs)*
What do you study / What's your major?	¿Qué estudias?	*(keh ehs-too-dyahs)*
What brings you here?	¿Qué te trae por aquí?	*(keh teh trah-eh pohr ah-kee)*
How long have you been here?	¿Cuánto tiempo llevas aquí?	*(kwahn-toh tyehm-poh yeh-bahr ah-kee)*
How do you know ___? (E.g. You might ask this if José is the mutual friend who introduced you, or the host of the event you're at.)	¿Cómo conoces a ___?	*(koh-moh koh-noh-sehs ah ___)*
Who do you know here?	¿A quién conoces aquí?	*(ah kyehn koh-noh-sehs ah-kee)*

81

Who are you here with?	¿Con quién estás aquí?	*(cohn kyehn eh-stahs ah-kee)*
Do you come here often?	¿Vienes seguido por aquí?	*(beh-neer seh-gwee-doh pohr ah-kee)*
Do you have any siblings/childr en?	¿Tienes hermanos/hijo s?	*(tyeh-nehs ehr-mah-nohs/ee-hohs)*
How old are they?	¿Qué edad tienen?	*(keh ehdahd tyeh-nehn?)*
What do your parents do?	¿Qué hacen tus padres?	*(keh ah-seeh toohs pah-drehs)*
Where did you grow up?	¿Donde creciste?	*(dohn-deh kreh-see-steh)*
Do you see your grandparents often?	¿Ves a tus abuelos a menudo?	*(Vehs ah toohs ah-bweh-lohs ah meh-noo-doh)*
Are you close with your parents?	¿Eres cercano/a sus padres?	*(eh-rehs sehr-kah-noh/nah ah soohs pah-drehs)*
What's your hometown like?	¿Cómo es tu pueblo natal?	*(coh-moh ehs too pweh-bloh nah-tahl)*
Do you have any pets?	¿Tienes alguna mascota?	*(tyeh-nehs ahl-goo-nah mahs-koh-tah)*
What breed is your dog/cat?	¿Qué raza es tu perro/gato?	*(keh rrah-sah ehs too peh-rroh/gah-toh)*

Continuing the Conversation

At what time shall we meet up?	¿A qué hora quedamos?	*(ah keh oh-rah keh-dah-mos)*
Is nine o'clock good for you?	¿Te viene bien a las nueve?	*(teh byeh-neh byehn ah lahs noo-eveh)*
That's good / That's not good for me	Me viene bien / No me viene bien	*(meh byeh-neh byehn / noh meh byeh-neh byehn)*
Where shall we meet up?	¿Dónde quedamos?	*(dohn-deh keh-dah-mos)*
How about if …?	¿Qué te parece si …?	*(keh teh pahr-ehseh see…)*
… we meet up tomorrow evening	… quedamos mañana por la noche	*(…keh-dah-mos mah-nyah-nah pohr lah noh-che)*
… we go out tonight	… salimos esta noche	*(… sahl-eeh-mohs eh-stah noh-che)*
Why don't we …?	¿Por qué no …?	*(pohr keh noh…)*
… have a coffee	… tomamos un café	*(… toh-mah-mos oon kah-feh)*
… have a few drinks in a bar	… nos tomamos unas copas en un bar	*(…nohs toh-mah-mos oo-nahs koh-pahs ehn oon bar)*
Do you feel like …?	¿Te apetece …?	*(teh ah-peh-teh-seh…)*
… meeting up this evening	… quedar esta noche	*(…keh-dahr ehs-tah noh-che)*
… going out for something to eat / drink	… salir a tomar algo	*(…sah-leer ah toh-mahr al-goh)*

We could …	Podríamos …	*(poh-dree-ah-mos…)*
… go to a concert	… ir a un concierto	*(eer ah oon kohn-syehr-toh)*
… go to a karaoke bar	… ir a un karaoke	*(eer ah oon kah-rah-oh-keh)*
Ok	Vale / Venga	*(bah-leh)*
Great	Perfecto	*(pehr-fehk-toh)*
That sounds good	Me parece bien	*(meh pah-reh-seh byehn)*
Fine	Muy bien	*(mwee byehn)*
I'm sorry, but I can't	Lo siento, pero no puedo	*(loh syehn-toh, peh-roh noh pweh-doh)*
I'd love to, but I can't	Me encantaría, pero no puedo	*(meh ehng-kahn-tah-ree-ah, peh-roh noh pweh-doh)*
Something has come up	Me ha surgido algo	*(meh ah surh-eedoh ahl-goh)*
I really don't feel like it	No me apetece mucho	*(noh meh apehteceh moo-choh)*
Today's not good for me	Me viene mal hoy	*(meh vyeh-neh mahl ohy)*
I'm busy	Estoy ocupado/ocupada	*(eh-stoy oh-koo-pah-doh/dah)*
Let's do it another day	Lo dejamos para otro día	*(loh deh-hamohs pah-rah oh-troh dee-ah)*
Don't worry / Never mind	No importa / No pasa nada / No te preocupes	*(noh im-pohr-tah / noh pah-sah nah-dah / noh teh preh-oh-koo-pehs)*
What a pity	Que pena	*(keh peh-nah)*

Sorry I am late	Perdona que haya llegado tarde	*(pehr-doh-nah keh ayah yegah-doh tahr-deh)*
You look amazing!	¡Estás guapísimo/gua písima!	*(ehs-tahs gwah-pee-see-moh/mah)*
What would you like to drink / eat?	¿Qué quieres beber / comer?	*(keh kyeh-rehs neh-ber / coh-mehr)*
I'll pay	Ya pago	*(yah pah-goh)*
Let's pay halves	Paguemos a medias	*(pah-geh-mos ah meh-dyahs)*
How much do I owe you?	¿Cuánto le debo?	*(kwahn-toh leh deh-boh)*
Is this seat taken?	¿Está desocupada esta silla?	*(ehs-tah dehs-oh-koo-pah-doh ehs-tah seyah)*
Do you know what the time is?	¿Sabe qué hora es?	*(sah-beh keh ah-oh-rah ehs?)*
Do you know what time this place closes?	¿Sabe a qué hora cierra este lugar?	*(sah-beh ah keh ah-oh-rah seh-rrahr ehs-teh loo-gahr)*
Do you know where the ___ is?	¿Sabe dónde está el/la ___?	*(sah-beh dohn-deh ehs-tah ehl/lah*
Do you like to travel?	¿Te gusta viajar?	*(teh goo-stah byah-hahr)*
What's your favorite place you've been to	¿Cuál es el lugar favorito en que has estado?	*(kwahl ehs ehl loo-gar fah-boh-ree-toh ehn keh ehs-tadoh)*
Which countries have you been to?	¿En qué países has estado?	*(ehn keh pay-ee-sehs ahs eh-sta-doh)*

| Have you been to [Rome]? | ¿Has estado en [Roma]? | *(ahs eh-stah-doh ehn [Roh-mah])* |
| Would you like to go to [Barcelona]? | ¿Querrías ir a [Barcelona]? | *(keh-rree-yahs eerh ah Bahr-seh-loh-nah)* |

If you could travel anywhere, where would you go?	Si pudieras viajar a cualquier lugar, ¿dónde viajarías?	*(see puh-dyeh-rahs vyah-har ah kwahl-kyehr loog-ahr, dohn-deh vyah-heh-steh?)*
Do you speak any other languages?	¿Hablas otros idiomas?	*(ah-blahs oh-trohs ihd-ee-ohmahs?)*
Where was the last place you went on holiday?	¿A dónde fuiste la ultima vez de vacaciones?	*(ah dohn-deh fwys-teh lah uhl-tee-mah vehs deh vak-kahsy-ohn-ehs?*
When did you start learning [Spanish]?	¿Cuándo empezaste a aprender [español]?	*(kwahn-doh ehmp-ehs-ahs-teh ah ah-prehn-dehr [ehs-pan-yol])*
Why did you become a [doctor]?	¿Qué te hizo convertirte en [médico]?	*(keh teh yso cohn-vert-eer-teh ehn [mehd-ee-koh])*
Do you like your job?	¿Te gusta tu trabajo?	*(teh goos-tah too trah-ba-hoh)*
What do you like the most about your job?	¿Qué es lo que más te gusta de tu trabajo?	*(keh ehs loh keh mahs teh goos-tah deh too trah-bah-hoh)*

What's the most difficult thing about your job?	¿Qué es la cosa más difícil sobre tu trabajo?	*(keh ehs lah cohsah mahs dee-fee-seel soh-breh too trah-bah-hoh?)*
Did you go to university?	¿Fuiste a la universidad?	*(fwys-teh ah lah oo-ni-ver-sydahd)*
Did you enjoy it?	¿La disfrutaste?	*(lah dihs-fruh-tahs-teh)*
What advice would you give to someone who wants to become a [programmer]?	¿Qué consejo le darías a alguien que quiere-convertirse en [programador]?	*(keh cohn-seh-hoh leh dahryahs ah ahl-gyenhn keh kyehr-eh cohn-ver-teer-syahy ehn [proh-grahm-ah-dor])*
If you could go back in time, would you study [psychology] again?	¿Si pudieras volver atrás en el tiempo, estudias [psicología] de nuevo?	*(see pooh-dee-ehr-ahs bohl-behr ah-trahs ehn ehl tee-ehmp-oh, eh-stoo-dy-ahs [programa] deh noo-eh-boh?)*
Do you like to cook?	¿Te gusta cocinar?	*(teh goos-tah coh-synahr)*
What's your favourite food?	¿Cuál es tu comida favorita?	*(kwahl ehs too cohm-eedah fah-bohr-eetah)*
Do you like [nationality] food?	¿Te gusta la comida [nacionalidad]?	*(teh goos-tah lah cohm-eedah [nationality])*
Can you recommend me a good restaurant near here?	¿Puedes recomendarme una buena restaurante cerca de aquí?	*(pweh-dehs rek-oh-mehn-dahr oo-nah bweh-nah reh-stah-rahn-teh sehr-kah deh ah-kee)*

What do they eat in your country?	¿Qué comen en su país?	*(keh coh-mehn ehn soo pah-ees)*
What do you like to do for fun?	¿Qué haces para divertirte?	*(keh ah sehs pah rah dyver-teer-teh)*
Do you like to [read]?	¿Te gusta [leer]?	*(teh goos-tah [leh-ehr])*
What's your favourite type of music?	¿Cuál tipo de música te gusta más?	*(kwahl tee-poh deh moo-see-kah teh goos-tah mahs)*
What's your favourite [film/book/band]?	¿Cuál es tu [película / libro / banda] favorita?	*(kwahl ehs too [peh-lee-koo-lah / lee-broh / bahn-dah] fah-bor-ytah)*
Do you play an instrument?	¿Tocas un instrumento?	*(toh-kahs oon een-strah-mehn-toh)*
What's the worst film you've seen?	¿Cuál es la peor película que has visto?	*(kwahl ehs lah pehor pehlee-koo-lah keh ahs bee-stoh)*
Do you play a sport?	¿Practicas algún deporte?	*(prak-tee-kahs ahl-goon deh-port-eh)*
What team do you support?	¿De qué equipo eres?	*(deh keh eh-kypoh eh-rehs)*
Do you agree?	¿Estás de acuerdo?	*(ehs-tahs deh akwehr-doh)*
What do you think about ___?	¿Qué piensas tú sobre ___?	*(keh pee-ehn-sahs too soh-breh ___)*
Tell me more about ___.	Háblame/Cuéntame más de ___.	*(ah-blah-meh / kwehn-tah-meh mahs deh ___)*

If you don't mind me asking...	Si no te importa que te pregunte...	*(see noh teh ehm-pohr-tah keh teh preh-goon-teh...)*
Someone told me that...	Alguien me dijo que...	*(ahl-gyehn meh dyhoh keh...)*
I heard that...	Escuché que...	*(ehs-koo-cheh keh...)*
Would you agree that...?	¿Estás de acuerdo en que...?	*(ehs-tahs deh ah-kwer-doh ehn keh...)*

CHAPTER SIXTEEN
CONNECTORS IN CONVERSATION

Opening Connectors

That is a good question.	Esa es una buena pregunta.	*(eh-sah ehs oo-nah bweh-nah preh-goon-tah)*
That is such a difficult question.	Es una pregunta tan difícil.	*(ehs oo-nah preh-goon-tah tahn dee-fee-seel)*
Once upon a time, long ago.	Había una vez, hace mucho tiempo.	*(ah-bee-yah oon-ah vehs, ah-seh moo-choh tyehm-poh)*

Filler Connectors

understandably	naturalmente	*(nah-too-rahl-mehn-teh)*
frankly speaking	hablando francamente	*(ah-blahn-doh frahng-kah-mehn-teh)*
between you and me	entre nosotros	*(ehn-treh noh-soh-trohs)*
anyway	de todas maneras / de todas formas	*(deh toh-dahs mah-neh-rahs / fohr-mahs)*
well then	bueno, entonces / pues bien	*(bweh-noh, ehn-tohn-sehs / pwehs byehn)*
well, as a matter of fact	Bueno, de hecho	*(bweh-noh, deh eh-choh)*

how can I put it?	¿Cómo puedo decirlo?	*(coh-moh pweh-doh deh-seer-loh)*
I must say that	debo decir que	*(deh-boh deh-seer keh)*
firstly / secondly	en primer / segundo lugar	*(ehn pree-mehr / seh-goon-doh loo-gahr)*
I would like you to know that	quiero que sepas que	*(kyeh-roh keh seh-pahs keh)*
I am afraid that	temo que / tengo miedo de que	*(teh-moh keh / tehn-goh myeh-doh deh keh)*
now and then it seems to me that	entonces, me parece que	*(ehn-tohn-sehs, meh pah-reh-seh keh)*
after all	después de todo	*(dehs-pwehs deh toh-doh)*
as far as I am concerned	por lo que a mí respecta	*(pohr loh keh ah mee rrehs-pehk-tah)*
more and more	más y más / cada vez más	*(mahs ee mahs / cah-dah behs mahs*
actually	en realidad / realmente	*(ehn rreh-ah-lee-dahd / rreh-ahl-mehn-teh)*
all joking aside	bromas aparte	*(broh-mahs ah-pahr-teh)*
now seriously	en serio / seriamente	*(ehn seh-ryoh / seh-ryah-mehn-teh)*

Apologizing Connectors

don't be upset, but	no se moleste, pero...	*(noh seh moh-lehs-teh, peh-roh...)*
it was a slip of the tongue	fue un desliz de la lengua	*(fweh oon dehs-lees deh lah lehng-gwah)*
I said it by mistake	lo dije por equivocación	*(loh dee-heh pohr eh-kee-boh-kah-syohn)*
I am sorry that	lamento que / siento que	*(lah-mehn-toh / syehn-toh keh)*

Qualifying Connectors

it seems to me	me parece	*(meh pah-reh-seh keh)*
I presume that	supongo que / presumo que	*(soo-pohng-goh keh / preh-soo-moh keh)*
I hope that	espero que / confío en que	*(ehs-peh-roh keh / kohm-fyoh ehn keh)*
in my opinion	en mi opinion	*(ehn mee oh-pee-nyohn)*
if that is true	si eso es cierto / si eso es verdad	*(see, eh-soh ehs syehr-toh / see eh-soh ehs behr-dahd)*
I don't know exactly	no lo sé exactamente	*(noh loh seh ehk-sahk-tah-mehn-teh)*
I would like to think that	me gustaría pensar que	*(meh goos-tah-rryah pehn-sahr keh)*
the way I see it is that	mi punto de vista es	*(mee poon-toh deh bees-tah ehs)*

as you may know	como quizás sepa / cómo sabrá	*(coh-moh kee-sah seh-pah / coh-moh sah-brah*
if I understand correctly	si he entendido bien	*(see eh ehn-tehn-dee-doh byehn)*
as you already know	cómo ya sabe	*(coh-moh yah sah-beh)*
as far as I know	hasta donde yo sé	*(ah-stah dohn-deh yoh seh)*
I have the impression that	tengo la impresión de que	*(tehn-goh lah eem-preh-syohn deh keh)*
it is usually true that	normalmente, es verdad	*(nohr-mahl-mehn-teh, ehs behr-dahd)*
you never know, but	uno nunca sabe, pero	*(oo-noh noon-kah sah-beh, peh-roh)*
I haven't thought about it before, but	no había pensado en eso antes	*(noh ah-bee-ia pehn-sah-doh ehn eh-soh ahn-tehs)*
if I am not mistaken	si no estoy equivocado	*(see noh eh-stoy eh-kee-boh-kah-doh)*
I am not certain whether	no estoy seguro de si	*(noh eh-stoy seh-goo-roh deh see)*
That reminds me…	Eso me recuerda…	*(eh-soh meh rreh-kohrr-dahr)*
Speaking of which…	Hablando de eso…	*(ah-blahn-doh deh eh-soh)*
On another note…	Por otra parte…	*(pohr oh-trah pahr-teh)*
I'm changing the subject, but…	Estoy cambiando de tema, pero…	*(eh-stoy cahm-bee-ahn-doh deh teh-mah, peh-roh)*

I was wondering…	Me preguntaba…	*(meh preh-goon-tah-bah…)*
Let me tell you something	Te voy a decir una cosa…	*(teh boy ah deh-seer oo-nah coh-sah)*
Of course!	¡Por supuesto! / ¡Claro que si!	*(pohr soo-pwehs-toh / klah-roh keh see)*
Really? / Seriously?	¿En serio?	*(ehn seh-ryoh)*
Hey!	¡Oye!	*(oh-yeh)*
Oysters! (exclamation)	¡Ostras!	*(ohs-trah)*
Oh my god!	¡Dios mio!	*(dyohs mee-oh)*
Let's see…	A ver…	*(ah behr)*
No way! (Don't tell me!)	¡No me digas!	*(noh meh dee-gahs)*
Okay! ("Dale" is more common in the Americas.)	¡Vale!	*(bah-leh)*
As far as I know.	Qué yo sepa	*(keh yoh seh-pah)*
Literally "I say", but you can use this to correct yourself after you misspeak.	Digo…	*(dee-goh)*
I mean…/Or rather….	O sea…	*(oh seh-ah)*
You know?	¿Sabes?	*(sah-behr)*

| A question... | Una pregunta... | *(oo-nah preh-goon-tah)* |

CHAPTER SEVENTEEN
EMERGENCY SITUATIONS

General Complains

I feel unwell.	No me siento bien.	*(noh meh see-ehn-toh byehn)*
I feel ill.	Me siento mal.	*(meh see-ehn-toh mahl)*
I have a headache.	Me duele la cabeza.	*(meh dw-ehl-eh lah cah-bez-ah)*
I have a stomachache.	Me duele el estomago.	*(meh dw-ehl-eh ehl ehs-toh-mah-goh)*
Can you give me something for the pain?	¿Puede me da algo para el dolor?	*(pweh-dehs meh dah ahl-goh pah-rah ehl doh-lor)*
I have a temperature.	Tengo fiebre.	*(tehn-goh fyeh-breh)*
I feel dizzy.	Me mareo.	*(meh mah-reh-oh)*
I have been sick.	Vomité.	*(boh-mee-teh)*
I've been stung by a bee/wasp.	Una abeja/una avispa me picó.	*(meh ah-beh-hah/oo-nah ah-bees-pah meh pee-koh)*
She's allergic to...	Tiene alérgica a...	*(tyeh-neh uh-luhr-jihk ah...)*
His thumb is swollen.	Tiene el pulgar hinchado.	*(tyeh-neh ehl pool-gahr een-chah-doh)*
I have a toothache.	Tengo dolor de muelas.	*(tehn-goh doh-lor deh moo-leh-tahs)*
It is not serious.	No es grave.	*(noh ehs grah-beh)*

What the Doctor Might Say

What's the matter?	¿Qué hay?	*(keh ay)*
Here is a prescription for some pills.	He aquí una prescripción para algunas pastilla.	*(eh ah-kee oo-nah prehs-kreep-syohn pah-rah ahl-goo-nahs pahs-tee-yah)*
Take one, three times a day, after each meal.	Tomad una, tres veces al día, después de las comidas.	*(toh-mahn-doh oo-nah, trehs veh-sehs ahl dee-ah, dehs-pwehs deh lahs coh-mee-dahs)*
Is this the first time this has happened?	¿Es la primera vez que pasó?	*(ehs lah pree-meh-rah vehs keh pah-soh)*
I advise you to go to hospital.	Recomiendo que vaya al hospital.	*(rreh-koh-mee-en-doh keh bay-ahs ahl ohs-pee-tahl)*
The pharmacist opens at 8am.	La farmacia abre a las ocho de la mañana.	*(lah fahr-mah-syah ah-breh ah lahs oh-choh deh lah mah-nyah-nah)*

The Pharmacist

Do you have anything for a cold?	Tienes algo para un resfriado.	*(tyeh-nehs ahl-goh pah-rah oon rrehs-fryah-doh)*
I need some tissues.	Necesito algunas pañuelos de papel.	*(neh-seh-see-toh ahl-goo-nahs pah-nyweh-loh deh pah-pel)*

Can you recommend an insect repellant?	¿Puede recomendarme un repelente de insectos?	*(pweh-deh rreh-koh-mehn-dahr-meh oon rreh-peh-lehn-teh deh een-sehk-toh)*
My friend has sunburn.	Mi amigo sufre quemaduras del sol.	*(mee ah-mee-goh soo-freh keh-mah-doo-rah dehl sohl)*
Call the American Embassy.	Llame a la Embajada de los Estados Unidos	*(yah-meh ah lah ehm-bah-hah-dah deh lohs ehs-tah-dohs oo-nee-dohs)*
Can you call an ambulance?	Se puede llamar a una ambulancia?	*(seh pweh-deh yam-ah a oo-nah am-boo-lahn-syah)*
Where can I find a doctor?	Dónde puedo encontrar un médico?	*(don-deh pweh-doh en-con-trah oon meh-dee-koh)*
Where is the hospital?	Dónde está el hospital?	*(don-deh ehs-tah el os-pee-tal)*
Where is the closest pharmacy?	Dónde está la farmacia más próxima?	*(don-deh ehs-tah la far-mah-syah mas prohk-see-mah)*
What's wrong?	Qué pasa?	*(keh pah-sah)*
I have a pain here	Tengo un dolor aquí	*(ten-goh oon do-lor)*
Do you have anything for...	Tiene algo para...	*(tee-eh-neh al-goh pah-rah)*
I need insect repellent	Necesito repelente de insectos	*(neh-ce-see-toh re-peh-len-teh deh in-sec-tos)*

CHAPTER EIGHTEEN
DESCRIBING YOURSELF

Feelings

I feel..	Me siento...	*(meh see-en-toh...)*
I am...	Estoy...	*(ehs-toy...)*
Happy	Feliz	*(feh-lees)*
Scared	Asustado (m)/ Asustada (f)	*(ah-soos-tah-doh)*
Worried	Preocupado (m) /Preocupada (f)	*(preh-oh-koo-pah-doh)*
Embarra ssed	Avergonzado (m) / Avergonzada (f)	*(ah-behr-gohn-sah-doh)*
Angry	Molesto (m) /Molesta (f)	*(moh-lehs-toh)*
Depress ed	Deprimido (m) /Deprimida (f)	*(deh-pree-mee-doh)*
Confuse d	Confundido (m)/Confundida (f)	*(kohm-foon-dee-doh)*
Surprise d	Sorprendido (m) /Sorprendida (f)	*(sohr-prehn-dee-doh)*
Shy	Penoso (m)/ Penosa (f) / Tímido (m)/Tímida (f)	*(peh-noh-soh / tee-mee-doh)*
Sad	Triste	*(trees-teh)*
Tired	Cansado (m) /Cansada (f)	*(kahn-sah-doh)*
Excited	Emocionado (m) /Emocionada (f)	*(eh-moh-syoh-nah-doh)*

Nervous	Nervioso (m) /Nerviosa (f)	*(nehr-byoh-soh)*
In love	Enamorado (m) /Enamorada (f)	*(eh-nah-moh-rah-doh)*
Grumpy	Amargado (m) /Amargada (f)	*(ah-mahr-gah-doh)*
Moody/ Bad-tempere d	Malhumorado (m) /Malhumorada (f)	*(mahl-oo-moh-rah-doh)*
Desperat e	Desesperado (m) /Desesperada (f)	*(dehs-ehs-peh-rah-doh)*
Fascinat ed	Fascinado (m) / Fascinada (f)	*(fah-see-nahr)*
Passiona te	Apasionado (m) /Apasionada (f)	*(ah-pah-syoh-nah-doh)*
Exhaust ed	Exhausto (m) /Exhausta (f)	*(ehk-sows-toh)*

Questions About Emotion

How do you feel?	¿Cómo te sientes?	*(koh-moh teh syehn-tehs)*
How are you?	¿Cómo estás?	*(koh-moh ehs-tahs)*
How are you doing?	¿Cómo andas?	*(koh-moh ahn-dahs)*
Do you feel tired?	¿Te sientes cansado?	*(teh syehn-tehs kahn-sah-doh)*
What's wrong?	¿Qué te pasa? ¿Qué te sucede?	*(keh teh pah-sah? keh teh soo-seh-deh)*

(Nothing is wrong)	No me pasa nada	*(noh meh pah-sah nah-dah)*
(I feel bad)	Me siento mal	*(meh syehn-toh mahl)*

Helpful Phrasal Verbs

to start to, to begin	Echar a	*(eh-chahr ah)*
to stop (doing something)	Dejar de	*(deh-hahr deh)*
to have just (done something)	Acabar de	*(ah-kah-bahr deh)*
to return to	Volver a	*(bohl-behr ah)*
to be in the mood for/about to	Estar para	*(ehs-tahr pah-rah)*
to be about to/in favor of	Estar por	*(ehs-tahr pohr)*
to think about/have an opinion	Pensar de	*(pehn-sahr keh)*
to think of/direct thoughts toward	Pensar en	*(pehn-sahr ehn)*
to dream about	Soñar con	*(soh-nyahr kohn)*
to rely on/count on	Contar con	*(kohn-tahr kohn)*
to make fun of/laugh at	Reírse de	*(rreh-eer-seh deh)*
to be glad to	Alegrarse de	*(ah-leh-grahr-seh deh)*
to fall in love with	Enamorarse de	*(eh-nah-moh-rahr-seh deh)*

| to miss | Echar de menos | *(eh-chahr deh meh-nohs)* |

Helpful Adverbs

up / above	arriba	*(ah-rree-bah)*
inside	adentro	*(ah-dehn-troh)*
here	acá	*(ah-kah)*
there	allá	*(ah-yah)*
far	lejos	*(leh-hohs)*
behind	detrás	*(deh-trahs)*
underneath	debajo	*(deh-bah-hoh)*
outside	fuera	*(fweh-rah)*
behind	atrás	*(ah-trahs)*
down / below	abajo	*(ah-bah-hoh)*
outside	afuera	*(ah-fweh-rah)*
today	hoy	*(oy)*
tomorrow	mañana	*(mah-nyah-nah)*
last night	anoche	*(ah-noh-cheh)*
the night before last	anteanoche	*(ahn-teh-ah-noh-cheh)*
recently	recientemente	*(rreh-syehn-teh-mehn-teh)*
briefly	brevemente	*(breh-beh-mehn-teh)*
daily	diariamente	*(dyah-ryah-mehn-teh)*
still	todavía	*(toh-dah-bee-ah)*
never	nunca	*(noong-kah)*
occasionally	ocasionalmente	*(oh-kah-syoh-nahl-mehn-teh)*
now	ahora	*(ah-oh-rah)*
yesterday	ayer	*(ah-yehr)*

the day before yesterday	anteayer	*(ahn-teh-ah-yehr)*
previously	previamente	*(preh-byah-mehn-teh)*
currently	actualmente	*(ahk-twahl-mehn-teh)*
permanently	permanentemente	*(pehr-mah-nehn-teh-mehn-teh)*
frequently	frecuentemente	*(freh-kwehn-teh-mehn-teh)*
already	ya	*(yuh)*
always	siempre	*(syehm-preh)*
weekly	semanalmente	*(seh-mah-nahl-mehn-teh)*
very	muy	*(mwee)*
a lot	mucho	*(moo-choh)*
less	menos	*(meh-nohs)*
so much	tanto	*(tahn-toh)*
somewhat	algo	*(ahl-goh)*
too much	demasiado	*(deh-mah-syah-doh)*
a little	poco	*(poh-koh)*
more	más	*(mahs)*
enough	bastante	*(bahs-tahn-teh)*
not at all	nada	*(nah-dah)*
well	bien	*(byehn)*
better	mejor	*(meh-hohr)*
fast	rápido	*(rrah-pee-doh)*
quickly	rápidamente	*(rrah-pee-dah-mehn-teh)*
clearly	claramente	*(klah-rah-mehn-teh)*
beautifully	bellamente	*(beh-yah-mehn-teh)*
loudly	ruidosamente	*(rrwee-doh-sah-mehn-teh)*

sweetly	dulcemente	*(dool-seh-mehn-teh)*
seriously	seriamente	*(seh-ryah-mehn-teh)*
like this/this way	así	*(ah-see)*
badly	mal	*(mahl)*
worse	peor	*(pehor)*
slowly	lentamente	*(lehn-tah-mehn-teh)*
intelligently	inteligentemente	*(een-teh-lee-hehn-teh-mehn-teh)*
carefully	cuidadosamente	*(kwee-dah-doh-sah-mehn-teh)*
quietly	tranquilamente	*(trahng-kee-lah-mehn-teh)*
stupendously	estupendamente	*(ehs-too-pehn-dah-mehn-teh)*
voluntarily	voluntariamente	*(boh-loon-tah-ryah-mehn-teh)*
easily	fácilmente	*(fah-seel-mehn-teh)*
besides	además	*(ah-deh-mahs)*
before	adelante	*(ah-deh-lahn-teh)*
around	alrededor	*(ahl-reh-deh-dohr)*
often	a menudo	*(ah meh-noo-doh)*
before	antes	*(ahn-tehs)*
rather	en lugar	*(ehn loo-gahr)*
as soon as	apenas	*(ah-peh-nahs)*
hence	por lo tanto	*(pohr loh tahn-toh)*
still	aún	*(ah-oon)*
yet	todavía	*(toh-dah-bee-ah)*
within	dentro	*(dehn-troh)*
after	después	*(dehs-pwehs)*
shortly	en breve	*(ehn breh-beh)*
then	entonces	*(ehn-tohn-sehs)*

towards	hacia	*(ah-syah)*
till / until	hasta	*(ahs-tah)*
in the meantime	mientras tanto	*(myehn-trahs tahn-toh)*
nor / neither	ni	*(nee)*
soon	pronto	*(prohn-toh)*
perhaps	tal vez	*(tahl behs)*
so	tan / así	*(tahn / ah-see)*
late	tarde	*(tahr-deh)*
early	temprano	*(tehm-prah-noh)*
everyday	todos los días	*(toh-dohs lohs dee-ahs)*
usually	usualmente	*(oo-swahl-mehn-teh)*
generally	generalmente	*(heh-neh-rahl-mehn-teh)*
from time to time	de vez en cuando	*(deh behs ehn kwahn-doh)*
monthly	mensualmente	*(mehn-swahl-mehn-teh)*
seldom	pocas veces	*(poh-kahs beh-sehs)*
annually	anualmente	*(ah-nwahl-mehn-teh)*

Personality Traits

boring	aburrido	*(ah-boo-rree-doh)*
affectionate	afectuoso	*(ah-fehk-twoh-soh)*
agile	ágil	*(ah-heel)*
pleasant	agradable	*(ah-grah-dah-bleh)*
joyful	alegre	*(ah-leh-greh)*
kind	amable	*(ah-mah-bleh)*

ambitious	ambicioso	*(ahm-bee-syoh-soh)*
friendly	amigable	*(ah-mee-gah-bleh)*
loving	amoroso	*(ah-moh-roh-soh)*
passionate	apasionado	*(ah-pah-syoh-nah-doh)*
listless	apático	*(ah-pah-tee-koh)*
attentive	atento	*(ah-tehn-toh)*
sassy	atrevido	*(ah-treh-bee-doh)*
cautious	cauto	*(kow-toh)*
jealous	celoso	*(seh-loh-soh)*
cynical	cínico	*(see-nee-koh)*
coherent	coherente	*(koh-eh-rehn-teh)*
considerate	considerado	*(kohn-see-deh-rah-doh)*
shocked	consternado	*(kohns-tehr-nah-doh)*
cruel	cruel	*(krwehl)*
careful	cuidadoso	*(kwee-dah-doh-soh)*
curious	curioso	*(koo-ryoh-soh)*
weak	débil	*(deh-beel)*
dependent	dependiente	*(deh-pehn-dyehn-teh)*
depressed	deprimido	*(deh-pree-mee-doh)*
untidy	desaliñado	*(dehs-ah-lee-nyah-doh)*
distrustful	desconfiado	*(dehs-kohm-fyah-doh)*
inconsiderate	desconsiderado	*(dehs-kohn-see-deh-rah-doh)*
careless	descuidado	*(dehs-kwee-dah-doh)*
direct	directo	*(dee-rehk-toh)*
discreet	discreto	*(dees-kreh-toh)*
distant	distante	*(dees-tahn-teh)*
absent-minded	distraído	*(dees-trah-ee-doh)*

funny	divertido	*(dee-behr-tee-doh)*
sweet	dulce	*(dool-seh)*
polite	educado	*(eh-doo-kah-doh)*
efficient	eficiente	*(eh-fee-syehn-teh)*
selfish	egoísta	*(eh-goh-ees-tah)*
elegant	elegante	*(eh-leh-gahn-teh)*
annoyed	enfadado	*(ehm-fah-dah-doh)*
conceited	engreído	*(ehng-greh-ee-doh)*
intrusive	entrometido	*(ehn-troh-meh-tee-doh)*
excited	entusiasmado	*(ehn-too-syahs-mah-doh)*
eccentric	excéntrico	*(ehk-sehn-tree-koh)*
demanding	exigente	*(ehk-see-hehn-teh)*
fastidious	fastidioso	*(fahs-tee-dyoh-soh)*
reliable	fiable	*(fyah-bleh)*
cold	frío	*(free-oh)*
generous	generoso	*(heh-neh-roh-soh)*
amusing	gracioso	*(grah-syoh-soh)*
grumpy	gruñón	*(groo-nyohn)*
skillful	hábil	*(ah-beel)*
beautiful	hermoso	*(ehr-moh-soh)*
hysterical	histérico	*(ees-teh-ree-koh)*
slacker; idle	holgazán	*(ohl-gah-sahn)*
awful	horrible	*(oh-rree-bleh)*
imaginative	imaginativo	*(ee-mah-hee-nah-tee-boh)*
impatient	impaciente	*(eem-pah-syehn-teh)*
impulsive	impulsivo	*(eem-pool-sahr)*

independent	independiente	*(een-deh-pehn-dyehn-teh)*
naive	ingenuo	*(eeng-heh-nwoh)*
immature	inmaduro	*(een-mah-doo-roh)*
restless	inquieto	*(eeng-kyeh-toh)*
intelligent	inteligente	*(een-teh-lee-hehn-teh)*
interesting	interesante	*(een-teh-reh-sahn-teh)*
intolerant	intolerante	*(een-toh-leh-rahn-teh)*
bold	intrépido	*(een-treh-pee-doh)*
playful	juguetón	*(hoo-geh-tohn)*
clever	listo	*(lees-toh)*
mature	maduro	*(mah-doo-roh)*
mischievous	malicioso	*(mah-lee-syoh-soh)*
mean	malo	*(mah-loh)*
melancholic	melancólico	*(meh-lahng-koh-lee-koh)*
liar	mentiroso	*(mehn-tee-roh-soh)*
meticulous	meticuloso	*(meh-tee-koo-loh-soh)*
stingy	tacaño	*(tah-kah-nyoh)*
humble	modesto	*(moh-dehs-toh)*
nervous	nervioso	*(nehr-byoh-soh)*
proud	orgulloso	*(ohr-goo-yoh-soh)*
patient	paciente	*(pah-syehn-teh)*
peaceful	pacífico	*(pah-see-fee-koh)*
passionate	pasional	*(pah-syoh-nahl)*
thoughtful	pensativo	*(pehn-sah-tee-boh)*
lazy	perezoso	*(peh-reh-soh-soh)*
persevering	perseverante	*(pehr-seh-beh-rahn-teh)*
naughty	pícaro	*(pee-kah-roh)*

powerful	poderoso	*(poh-deh-roh-soh)*
positive	positivo	*(poh-see-tee-boh)*
practical	práctico	*(prahk-tee-koh)*
pretentious	pretencioso	*(preh-tehn-syoh-soh)*
provocative	provocador	*(proh-boh-kah-dohr)*
prudent	prudente	*(proo-dehn-teh)*
punctual	puntual	*(poon-twahl)*
fussy	quisquilloso	*(kees-kee-yoh-soh)*
realistic	realista	*(rreh-ah-lees-tah)*
quiet	reservado	*(rreh-sehr-bah-doh)*
responsible	responsable	*(rrehs-pohn-sah-bleh)*
ridiculous	ridículo	*(rree-dee-koo-loh)*
confident	seguro	*(seh-goo-roh)*
sensible	sensato	*(sehn-sah-toh)*
sensitive	sensible	*(sehn-see-bleh)*
serious	serio	*(seh-ryoh)*
helpful	servicial	*(sehr-bee-syahl)*
nice	simpático	*(seem-pah-tee-koh)*
honest	sincero	*(seen-seh-roh)*
dirty	sucio	*(soo-syoh)*
shallow	superficial	*(soo-pehr-fee-syahl)*
talented	talentoso	*(tah-lehn-toh-soh)*
shy	tímido	*(tee-mee-doh)*
silly	tonto	*(tohn-toh)*
clumsy	torpe	*(tohr-peh)*
cool	tranquilo	*(trahny-kee-loh)*
sad	triste	*(trees-teh)*
brave	valiente	*(bah-lyehn-teh)*

CHAPTER NINETEEN
GENERAL TOURISM

Going to a Museum

I would like to go to the...	Me gustaría ir a la...	*(meh goos-tah-ryah eer ah lah...)*
art museum	el museo de arte	*(moo-seh-oh deh ahr-teh)*
science museum	el museo de la ciencia	*(moo-seh-oh deh lah syehn-syah)*
natural history museum	museo de historia natural	*(moo-seh-oh deh ees-toh-ryah nah-too-rahl)*
What happened here?	¿Qué sucedió aquí?	*(keh soo-seh-dee-oh ah-kee)*
Who build this?	¿Quién construyó esto?	*(kyehn kohns-trw-yoh eh-steh)*
Who destroyed this?	¿Quién destruyó esto?	*(kyehn dehs-trw-yoh eh-steh)*
Where did this come from?	¿de dónde salió esto?	*(deh dohn-dyeh sah-lyoh eh-stoh)*
How old is this?	¿Qué edad tiene esto?	*(keh eh-dahd tyeh-neh eh-stoh)*
How many people visit here?	¿Cuántas personas visitan aquí?	*(kwhan-tahs pehr-soh-nahs bih-sy-tahn ah-kee)*

What attractions should I visit?	¿Qué atracciones debo visitar?	*(keh ah-trahk-syohn deh-boh bee-see-tahr)*
How long will it take to get there?	¿Cuánto tiempo se tardará en llegar?	*(kwahn-toh tyehm-poh seh tahr-dahr-ah ehn yeh-gahr)*
How long will it take to see it all?	¿Cuánto tiempo tomará verlo todo?	*(kwahn-toh tyehm-poh tahr-dahr-ah*

At the Beach

Do you want to go to the beach?	¿Quieres ir a la playa?	*(kyreh-rehs eer ah lah plahy-ah)*
Is there a restaurant near by?	¿Hay algún restaurante cerca?	*(ahy ahl-goon rrehs-tow-rahn-teh sehr-kah)*
Where can I buy sunscreen?	¿Dónde puedo comprar protector solar?	*(dohn-deh pweh-doh kohm-prahr pruh-tehk-duhr soh-lahr)*
How much does this umbrella cost?	¿Cuánto cuesta este paraguas?	*(kwahn-toh kwehs-tah eh-steh pahr-ahg-wahs)*
How much for a popsicle?	¿Cuánto por una paleta?	*(kwahn-toh pohr oo-nah pah-leh-tah)*
When is high tide?	¿Cuándo es la marea alta?	*(kwahn-doh ehs lah mah-reh-ah bah-ha)*
When is low tide?	¿Cuándo es la marea baja?	*(kwahn-doh ehs lah mah-reh-ah ahl-tah)*
Can I fish here?	¿Puedo pescar aquí?	*(pweh-doh pehs-kar ah-kee)*

Can I surf here?	¿Puedo surfear aquí?	*(pweh-doh soor-feh-ahr ah-kee)*
Are there any rocks?	¿Hay rocas?	*(ahy roh-kahs)*
Are there any coral reefs?	¿Hay arrecifes de coral?	*(ahy ah-rreh-see-feh deh koh-rahl)*
Are there any whales?	¿Hay ballenas?	*(ahy bah-yeh-nah)*

On a Day Hike

How long is this trail?	¿Cuánto dura este camino?	*(kwahn-toh doh-rah ehs-teh kah-mee-noh)*
How many kilometers are in a mile?	¿Cuantos kilometros hay en una milla?	*(kwahn-tohs kee-loh-meh-trohs ahy ehn oo-nah mylah)*
Where is the lookout?	¿Dónde está el mirador?	*(dohn-deh ehs-tah ehl myrah-dohr)*
How difficult is the hike?	¿Qué tan difícil es la caminata?	*(keh tahn dee-fee-seel ehs lah kah-mee-nah-tah)*
Do we have enough supplies?	¿Tenemos suficientes provisiones?	*(teh-neh-mos soo-fee-syehn-teh proh-bee-syoh-nehs)*
Which way do we go?	¿Hacia dónde vamos?	*(ah-syah dohn-deh vah-mos)*

CONCLUSION

Spanish is a beautiful and diverse language spoken from the jungles of Costa Rica to the salt flats of Bolivia and beyond. Learning the language, or simply holding onto this book, grants you more than comfort and safety in another country. Speaking Spanish allows you to connect with those around you, passing from tourist to welcomed friend within the span of a few sentences.

The technicalities of individual accents and the grammar behind the language will come in time. The most important thing to do is to practice—try these phrases and see how they work for you! From there, mix and match the vocabulary to create your own sentences. It's never too late to learn a new language! Take your time and don't feel pressured to speak perfectly; Spanish speakers are often amazingly hospitable and will be patient with you.

This book is a great way to ease your way into the language while abroad—not only have these phrases been handpicked by travelers in South America, Latin America, and Spain, but they have also been tailored to be as versatile and useful as possible. From getting to the hotel to ordering at the market, this book holds the conversational pieces needed for any interactions you have abroad. Do enjoy this experience without worries and make sure to sip the culture through its language. Enjoy your travels!

Printed in the USA
CPSIA information can be obtained
at www.ICGtesting.com
LVHW011024311223
767822LV00017BA/1859

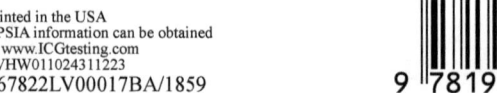